The New
Supply Chain
Agenda

The New Supply Chain Agenda

The Five Steps That Drive Real Value

Reuben E. Slone

J. Paul Dittmann

John T. Mentzer

HARVARD BUSINESS PRESS

BOSTON, MASSACHUSETTS

Library of Congress Cataloging-in-Publication Data

Slone, Reuben E.
  The new supply chain agenda : the 5 steps that drive real value / Reuben E. Slone, J. Paul Dittmann, John T. Mentzer.
    p. cm.
  ISBN 978-1-4221-4936-2 (hbk. : alk. paper)
  1. Business logistics.   I. Dittmann, J. Paul.   II. Mentzer, John T. III. Title.
  HD38.5.S575 2010
  658.7—dc22

                                                    2009038627

CONTENTS

1

Focus on Supply Chain as the Driver of Shareholder Value

CHANCES ARE, IF YOU HAVE picked up this book, you already feel that your supply chain is not delivering excellence, or that it could deliver more. Given the economic pressures brought on by the end of cheap energy, the increasingly global nature of manufacturing and retail competition, and the worldwide Great Recession of 2008–2010, you probably are also looking for ways to unlock capital within your organization as an alternative to equity and debt.

We have written this book to be as free of jargon as possible so that it can be read by anyone interested in learning more about the new supply chain agenda. But we have targeted it especially for the senior supply chain professional. Perhaps you are looking for a way to move your supply chain to the next level. Perhaps you know the tremendous potential power of your supply chain, but are frustrated with how slowly your company is moving to realize that full potential. Either way, we assure you that this book will help you unlock true supply chain excellence in your firm and provide a sustainable way to reduce inventory and costs, while increasing customer-order fill rates. These actions will translate into balance sheet, income statement, and cash flow improvements that together yield more *economic profit* for the firm. As we will show, economic profit connects supply chain excellence directly to shareholder value.

The goal of this book is *not* to convince you that you can make these improvements. Our goal is to show you how to achieve them. We should know, since we have had to do it ourselves and have discovered, sometimes the hard way, the basic elements along the pathway linking supply chain excellence, economic profit, and shareholder value. Together we have had long careers in industry and academia. We have had to deliver supply chain excellence, and we have seen others do it as well. Collectively, our experience has put us in contact with hundreds of companies, many of which have come to the University of Tennessee for in-depth supply chain audits or have attended the supply chain forum sponsored by the university. Stories from those audits and forum contacts have been collected into a database of five hundred companies from which we drew the examples, stories, and quotes used throughout the book. (See "Source of Examples.")

What You Will Learn in Each Chapter

In this chapter, we will explain how to focus your supply chain team on what is most important to your firm: growing shareholder value. It will help you translate your initiatives into the language of the boardroom and get the priority you need. Chapter 2 guides

Source of Examples

In this book, we illustrate concepts with many examples and stories. We have drawn those from our interactions with hundreds of companies, both as professionals and consultants. Unless otherwise noted, stories, examples, and quotations in this book derive from the five-hundred-company database at the University of Tennessee, which houses details from supply chain audits conducted by the university, as well as interactions with attendees of the university's annual supply chain forum.

---

you in laying out the five steps to achieve supply chain excellence in your company. The path begins with the creation of a supply chain strategy. We strongly believe that this strategy needs to include the five steps which we introduce in chapter 2 and then explain thoroughly throughout the rest of the book. Chapter 2 also includes a self-test to evaluate where you stand now in your journey. Chapter 3 describes the first of the five steps—hiring talent. If you don't have the right people in place, you can't build and execute an appropriate strategy. You will see how finding talent for supply chain positions has unique challenges due largely to the cross-functional and cross-company process challenges supply chain executives face. Chapter 4 describes the next step along the pathway, which is the choice and implementation of the right supply chain technology. Improperly understood or implemented, technology can cause severe damage rather than improvement. You must be careful in selecting and applying technology. In this chapter, you will find the things to do and avoid. Chapter 5 shows how each function in your firm plays a critical role in a successful supply chain and will help you develop a clear vision for how functions work together to achieve supply chain excellence. In addition, at the end of the chapter, an assessment test helps you honestly evaluate your process for aligning your company's demand and supply sides. Chapter 6 focuses on how your company can achieve breakthough results by collaborating externally. You should pay special attention to the best practices for working together with suppliers and customers. Chapter 7 addresses the last but equally critical step toward a strategy for supply chain excellence—change management. Everything else is for naught if you don't execute successfully. This chapter will give you practical advice on how to increase your chances of success. Chapter 8 provides detailed case studies of two companies we were involved with—a manufacturer, Whirlpool, and a retailer, Stage Stores. Each firm developed and then executed a supply chain strategy that delivered excellence, economic profit, and shareholder value. In both cases, we had more than front-row views of the considerable challenges; we were actually part of the teams that drove the results.

Driving Shareholder Value with Your Supply Chain

Given the hype of the last ten years surrounding the supply chain excellence of companies such as Walmart, Toyota, and Amazon, why do so many firms still not get it? The success of the firms ranked in AMR Research's Supply Chain Top 25, such as Apple, IBM, and Procter & Gamble, should have made everyone focus on supply chain as the driver of shareholder value.[1] We hear a lot about the importance of supply chain, but actions often do not match words.

The most neglected pathway to increasing shareholder value runs through the supply chain. This isn't a cost-cutting argument, though supply chain excellence often dramatically reduces costs over the long term. In fact, reaching excellence is expensive, both in terms of executive attention and actual cash outlays. Supply chain excellence drives shareholder value because it controls the heartbeat of the firm—the fundamental flow of materials and information from suppliers through the firm to its customers. Unfortunately, too many companies have a supply chain in which this flow is crippled by the lack of a strategy, the absence of talent, a misapplication of technology, internal and external silos, and a basic lack of discipline in managing change, all issues we address in later chapters.

In company after company, we see behavior that is inconsistent with this expansive idea of the supply chain function. Yet this broader view has been around for years (see "Standard Definition of "Supply Chain").

When we mention supply chain in this book, we refer to *the activity that manages the flow of information, money, and material across the extended enterprise, from supplier through the functional silos of the firm to customer*. This book generally does not cover manufacturing; its focus is on the supply chain outside the four walls of the plant.

The supply chain isn't just trucks, pallets, and warehouses. But being trapped in a traditional view is one of the primary reasons

---

Standard Definition of *Supply Chain*

The Council of Supply Chain Management Professionals (CSCMP) defines the supply chain as encompassing the planning and management of all activities involved in sourcing and procurement, conversion, and all logistics management activities. Importantly, it also includes coordination and collaboration with channel partners, which can be suppliers, intermediaries, third-party service providers, and customers. In essence, supply chain management integrates supply and demand management within and across companies.

that few companies are taking advantage of the shareholder value opportunity presented by supply chain excellence. You, like many executives we talk to, may be skeptical that investing in this new, expansive vision of a supply chain is worth it. So we'll begin by looking at the unequivocal link between supply chain excellence and shareholder value by focusing first on *economic profit*, which is the linchpin between the two.

Driving Shareholder Value by Creating Economic Profit

Economic profit very simply is *profit less the cost of capital needed to generate that profit.* That profit is a big deal because it means the company is delivering returns above the cost of the capital invested. Generating economic profit should be the prime goal of all firms. Most CEOs intuitively know that economic profit drives shareholder value. *But many don't clearly comprehend the linkage that begins at supply chain excellence and continues to shareholder value via economic profit.* Supply chain excellence very often can deliver the most upside to economic profit and shareholder value because its full potential has been so underutilized in the past compared to other corporate initiatives.

Economic Profit Increases Shareholder Value

When economic profit increases over time, shareholder value increases. Stern Stewart & Co. has done extensive research on this concept which it calls economic value added (EVA). It has shown through analysis in many companies that the relationship is very strong, especially over time, when the data is normalized.[2]

To understand the impact of economic profit, consider the following example: suppose a newly formed company earned $10 million in net income on a capital base of $100 million. This capital base includes both physical capital, like factories and warehouses, and working capital, like inventory and receivables.[3] In this simple example, the company has a return on capital of 10 percent. However, suppose the required return that investors demand for having their money locked into this new venture adds up to an investment expectation of 13 percent on the invested capital. That means that, although this firm is enjoying accounting profits, it actually lost 3 percent last year for its shareholders compared to their expectations. Economic profit charges the company a penalty for tying up investors' cash to support operations. The capital on the balance sheet becomes just as important as the net income on the income statement.

As Peter Drucker said, in a *Harvard Business Review* article, "Unless a business returns a profit that is greater than its cost of capital, it operates at a loss."[4] Interviews we conducted with stock market analysts from several different investment firms substantiate Drucker's view. They confirm that the price of a firm's stock depends on whether investors see it earning a good return over its cost of capital over time, that is, a good economic profit.[5]

The Supply Chain Drives Economic Profit

In an increasing but still small number of firms, the CEO and the board understand the value of the supply chain to their firm. But many other CEOs, battered by an immense range of items competing for their attention, do not see this link clearly. Yet the link is there. Using the expansive view of the supply chain described earlier, in many firms, the supply chain controls most of the inventory, manages 60 percent to 70 percent of the cost, is the foundation to generate revenue by providing outstanding product availability, and manages most of the physical assets of the firm (see figure 1-1).

We believe the Great Recession of 2008–2010 will increase the focus on economic profit. In an era of tighter credit, supply chain levers can be used to free cash reserves from balance sheets rather

FIGURE 1-1

How changes in revenue, cost, working capital, and physical capital flow into economic profit and shareholder value

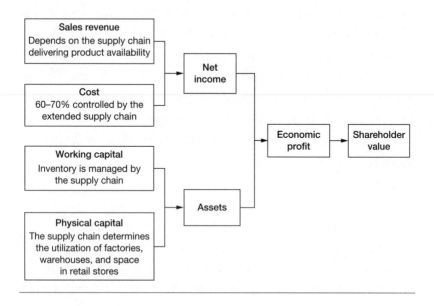

than depending on restricted credit markets. The opportunity to increase shareholder value in the future will be to take care of both the income statement and balance sheet through supply chain excellence.

Creating Economic Profit at a Retail Chain

The savvy CEO of a major department store chain, when asked by his executive vice president of supply chain what he expected the function to deliver, said, "I want the highest possible availability with the lowest inventory investment and lowest possible logistics cost." With this simple, direct statement, the CEO focused the organization simultaneously on the key elements of economic profit, namely revenue growth, cost reduction, and low asset utilization. The executive vice president translated his CEO's direction into three broad objectives for the organization:

1. Drive high customer-order fill rates, reducing out-of-stock products to generate more revenue (move from 95 percent to 99 percent).

2. Achieve that goal with low inventory levels to improve cash flow (reduce inventory 30 percent over the next 18 months).

3. Achieve it with excellent cost productivity to increase profit margins (cut cost 10 percent).

Higher sales, increased margins, and more cash flow with lower capital invested form a pretty effective recipe for increasing economic profit. The real question is, how can the supply chain deliver on these three broad objectives?

The supply chain managers in this company asked themselves what levers they could pull to achieve the executive vice president's objectives. After much debate and analysis, they came up with the set of major initiatives for the next eighteen months:

- *Reduce stock-keeping units (SKUs).* The company carried nearly fifteen thousand SKUs of different types of products in its stores. The managers set a specific goal to drive a 25 percent reduction in slow-moving SKUs, and they planned to visibly track progress every month.

- *Improve forecasting.* They made forecast accuracy an important goal for sales and marketing, as well as the forecasting group. Measuring forecast accuracy using mean absolute percent error (MAPE), they set a goal to cut error by 25 percent.[6]

- *Increase frequency of store replenishment in a low-cost way.* The managers planned to go from one store-replenishment delivery per week to three deliveries per week, and they planned to revise their network flow and their *private fleet to do this for only a 15 percent increase in cost*, even though they planned tripling store deliveries. With more deliveries, they expected to greatly improve product availability to support revenue growth.

- *Improve inventory accuracy.* In both the stores and the warehouses, they planned to put in place a more disciplined cycle process to randomly count small amounts of inventory in the warehouse continuously over the year to improve accuracy from 98 percent to 99.5 percent.

- *Manage new product transitions in a world-class manner.* The managers resolved to follow a stage-gate process to introduce new products put in place two years earlier (we describe stage gates fully in chapter 5). They planned to involve the supply chain deeply in all of the key decisions.

- *Collaborate aggressively with suppliers.* They chose their top-ten suppliers and planned to openly share information on forecasts and strategy, set joint metrics, and launch specific joint initiatives to improve such activities as damage and on-time delivery.

At the end of the eighteen-month period, these initiatives produced impressive results, which the team documented carefully. In some cases, as shown in table 1-1, they exceeded their goal, and in others, they fell slightly short.

But what about the overarching objectives dealing with cost, inventory, and availability? Were the projects summarized in the table truly the right levers required to deliver the fundamental components of economic profit? The managers were indeed able to celebrate success, with customer-order fill rates improving from 91 percent to 98 percent, inventory falling $175 million or 24 percent, and total cost as a percentage of sales declining by 8 percent or $28 million. The team later agreed that the fill-rate improvement yielded at least $75 million more in revenue, which yielded $36 million more in net income (cost reduction plus the

TABLE 1-1

Results of a retail company's supply chain excellence initiatives

Initiative	Goal	Actual after 18 Months
Reduce SKUs	25 percent reduction	15 percent
Improve forecast accuracy	25 percent MAPE improvement	28 percent
Increase delivery frequency	300 percent increase in deliveries at a 15 percent cost increase	300 percent increase at an 18 percent cost increase
Improve inventory accuracy	Improve to 99.5 percent	99.8 percent
Manage new product transitions	Follow stage-gate process and involve supply chain	Improved, but still a gap
Collaborate with suppliers	Collaboration activities with top 10 suppliers	Collaboration activities with 7 suppliers accomplished

income from the increased sales). The net income increase of $36 million along with the working capital decrease of $175 million yielded a major increase in economic profit (net income minus the cost of capital).

The team knew that although accomplishing these initiatives was challenging, maintaining the change as a permanent way of life would be the real driver of sustained economic profit increases over time. The firm continued gradual improvement for the next two years and now is wrestling with how to raise the bar and move performance to an even higher level.

The Link Between Shareholder Value and Supply Chain Excellence

World-class supply chains create economic profit when they:

- Support higher *revenue* by providing flawless delivery to customers.

- Reduce *cost* through ever more efficient operations.

- Reduce *capital* requirements with lower inventory, overall working capital, and streamlined physical networks.

Effective supply chain management means driving enterprise cross-functional integration to produce the highest availability with the minimum cost and capital investment. This increases economic profit because it supports higher revenue at lower costs and with lower working capital. An increase in economic profit supports an increase in shareholder value.

In the 1990s, the relationship between supply chain excellence and shareholder value was not well understood. For example, Gary Balter, managing director of Credit Suisse, observed that few analysts likely appreciated the major change that occurred at Target in the late 1990s and early 2000s, when Target went from a distribution system clogged with slow-turning merchandise to a flow-through system, with distribution centers dedicated to carry fast-turning merchandise.[7] Balter observed that this resulted in a major reduction in inventory, with improved product availability. But as appreciation of its improving supply chain grew, so did its relative stock market improvement versus Walmart and Kmart. Interestingly, when Walmart later began its Remix supply chain program, all stock market analysts focused on it. Walmart highlighted Remix because, by then, analysts and Wall Street had begun to appreciate the positive impact and importance of the supply chain. More CEOs and boards are now taking notice due to stock analysts' consistent questions regarding the state of firms' supply chains and Wall Street's reward for supply chain performance.

As another confirmation of the link of company performance to supply chain excellence, Credit Suisse identified firms that, based on its analysis, have leading versus underperforming supply chains. Then it compared them to the return on invested capital and margins. Figure 1-2 shows the results of their analysis and illustrates the benefit of supply chain excellence.

FIGURE 1-2

Companies with leading supply chain systems have higher operating margins and outperform other retailers

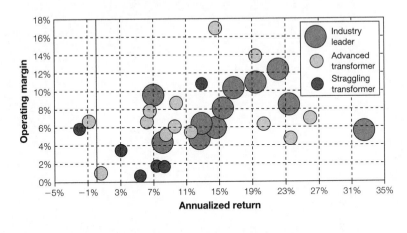

Source: Company data, Credit Suisse estimates. Used with permission.

In order to further gauge the increase in earnings and stock performance due to supply chain excellence, the Credit Suisse analysis in table 1-2 looks at several companies that were successful in transforming their supply chains. It also quantifies the benefits that stragglers could realize should they embark on that mission successfully. For Nordstrom, Michaels, Best Buy, J.C. Penney, and Target, there is an average improvement in operating margins of 518 basis points, an average increase of 17 percent in inventory turns, and a 20 percent increase in sales per square foot.

How One Manufacturer Drove
Higher Economic Profit

There are other ways to generate economic profit, including new products, new marketing programs, acquisitions, and simply squeezing cost and assets. Most firms have worked these

TABLE 1-2

Credit Suisse's analysis of the impact, real or potential, of supply chain excellence on various retail chains

	ANNUALIZED RETURNS		OPERATING MARGIN			INVENTORY TURNS			GROSS MARGIN PER SQUARE FOOT			SALES PER SQUARE FOOT		
	Total	Relative	Prior	After	BPS Increase	Prior	After	Increase	Prior	After	Increase	Prior	After	Increase
Nordstrom	33.1%	25.2%	2.6%	10.6%	804	4.1x	5.5x	33%	$121	$171	42%	$340	$437	28%
Michaels	20.6%	7.4%	5.7%	10.4%	470	2.4x	2.7x	13%	$61	$81	32%	$184	$216	17%
Best Buy	28.1%	17.3%	3.6%	5.6%	200	7.8x	7.4x	-6%	$212	$238	13%	$938	$951	1%
J.C. Penney	34.7%	26.8%	3.1%	9.7%	660	2.2x	3.3x	53%	$57	$76	33%	$171	$193	13%
Target	10.0%	2.9%	3.9%	8.5%	458	7.2x	6.5x	-9%	$69	$108	58%	$227	$321	41%
Average	25%	16%	Average		518	Average		17%	Average		35%	Average		20%

Source: Company data, Credit Suisse estimates, Bloomberg.

*Total returns relative to the S&P 500 retailing index.

approaches to death for years. The supply chain is often a new horse to ride, with huge potential. Consider one company that had tried everything to increase shareholder value. In desperation, the CEO and CFO turned to their supply chain.

The CEO and CFO of a *Fortune* 150 manufacturer of consumer durable goods had a problem. They were returning from the latest quarterly results conference call, still smarting from the beating they had received for the sorry state of cash flow in the corporation. Even though net income was excellent, the cash flow and economic profit were disappointing to investors. They knew they had to take aggressive action fast, not only to support the stock price, but for the long-term viability of the company. They decided to implement a creative and radically different plan to increase cash flow. For several months, they had been debating whether to use their supply chain organization as the catalyst to drive down working capital and improve cash flow. They realized that the time for debate had passed.

The CFO hurried to his office and placed a call to the vice president of supply chain and the vice president of manufacturing requesting a quick meeting. When the four gathered, the CEO and the CFO shared with them the critical need to generate more cash flow. They said they wanted to try something totally different. The plan was to leverage the company's supply chain to drastically reduce working capital. The firm had nearly $1.2 billion of cash tied up in working capital. The executives issued an extreme challenge: cut working capital by 50 percent and do it using improvements in the supply chain. And there was one more thing . . . do it within twenty-four months.

When the CFO gave this assignment, the supply chain and manufacturing vice presidents looked at each other and realized they both were thinking the same thing, "I wish I could remember the definition of working capital, but I'm too embarrassed to ask right now!" Obviously, the project had a humble beginning, but the firm accomplished the stretch goal. Leveraging its supply chain, the company reduced working capital by half and managed to free $600 million in cash. Side benefits led to reductions in operating cost and improvements in availability, as they managed to hit on all cylinders of economic profit. But it was far from easy.

Working capital has been called "the capital that doesn't work." It just sits there as inventory and receivables and consumes the company's cash. Any business is much healthier with its assets in motion. From the supply chain perspective, a more descriptive term for working capital is cash-to-cash cycle time, or asset velocity.

Overall, working capital for most firms consists of four components or "buckets": (1) finished-goods inventory; (2) raw and work-in-process inventory; (3) accounts payable; and (4) accounts receivable. Put another way, working capital is essentially total inventory plus receivables minus payables.

With the working capital goal set, the company formed a supply chain working capital team to create a strategy for accomplishing the goal. The team members launched projects in each of the four buckets, starting with their comfort zone—finished-goods inventory. They created a detailed plan to rationalize finished inventory to 50 percent of its current level, a $250 million reduction, without negatively affecting product availability.

1. Finished-Goods Inventory

The inventory reduction plan depended on four tasks:

1. Cut the number of SKUs in order to manage inventory across fewer finished products.

2. Improve manufacturing flexibility to react faster to demand changes.

3. Address slow-moving inventory—30 percent of the inventory was just plain not selling—and create a

product segmentation strategy allowing fast-moving SKUs to carry the highest inventories. (Prior to this initiative, profitability suffered because customers of fast-moving SKUs were served with the same inventory levels as slow-moving ones.)

4. Manage demand to more perfectly match the abilities of the supply chain. The goal here was to drive inventories to a bare minimum by managing demand to levels that could be quickly met by flexible manufacturing plants and logistics. This required new internal cross-functional collaboration, with sales, marketing, manufacturing, and logistics all pulling in the same direction, requiring significant cultural changes.

All four of these initiatives required radically new thinking and cross-functional cooperation. Fortunately, the CEO provided the leadership and support the team needed to succeed.

SKU and Product Complexity Management

The team members knew that the firm had a lot of inventory spread across thousands of models, and even worse, they knew they had no formal process for killing off old, underperforming SKUs. Most firms ignore slow-moving and obsolete SKUs, sometimes for years. Management doesn't want to think about it, knowing that it's going to mean margin cuts to get rid of the stuff. But eventually, the company must deal with it, if for no other reason than the huge amount of warehouse space consumed. In a panic, firms then typically launch a program to rid themselves of the offending merchandise, generally by marking it down or scrapping it. This process, like the seasons, repeats without end.

This firm was no exception. The team members realized the only permanent fix was to install a monthly process to remove underperforming SKUs, writing off small amounts regularly versus large amounts under duress. They also knew from past experience that the supply chain organization as it existed could never success-fully lead an SKU-reduction project. They could do a great analysis, but simply did not have the power to cut SKUs. SKU management was the realm of the marketing department. So they handed this piece of the project over to the vice president of marketing, though the CEO demanded regular reports on progress.

First, the working capital team members adopted a goal of a 25 percent reduction in SKUs. They then allocated that goal across all of the individual product/brand combinations in the firm. As an aid in carrying out the SKU reduction, the team then determined the cost of carrying an SKU (see table 1-3).

TABLE 1-3

The cost of an SKU

Category	Cost element
Manufacturing costs	Changeovers
	Schedule change costs
	Component part management
	Unique tool maintenance
	Work-in-process inventory management
	Overhead to manage added complexity
Logistics costs	Warehousing and facility costs
	Inventory management
	Overhead to manage complexity
Sales and marketing costs	Training
	Communications
	Closeouts
Procurement	Supply base management
	Materials management
Design engineering	Developing and maintaining design specs
	Testing
Customer	Warehouse space
	Storage space
	Display changes
	Inventory holding cost

The firm found that just the manufacturing and logistics costs alone totaled over $100,000 for each SKU. Surprised and shocked at the cost, the team members decided to take aggressive action. To control this cost, they knew they had to cut SKUs and then maintain the progress. This led to installing a set of automated decision rules:

1. When an SKU's sales fell below a target threshold of a hundred units sold in the last quarter, it automatically transferred to a "watch list."

2. After thirty more days, it then was reclassified as "discontinued," but with the same pricing still in effect.

3. After another thirty days, its classification moved to "obsolete," with an automatic price reduction of 20 percent.

4. Every month, the price was automatically reduced by another 20 percent.

5. At somewhere around the 40 percent to 60 percent price level, if any product still remained, it was scrapped, donated to charity, or placed on an eBay auction.

Now they had a process to flush out unproductive SKUs at their end of life. But that was only half the battle. They also needed discipline at the *beginning* of life. For this, they added a "add one–cut one" corporate policy that required an old SKU to be retired whenever a new one was introduced, unless extensive justification occurred.

Of course, getting rid of obsolete SKUs meant eliminating the inventory that went along with those SKUs. Some supply chain managers tell us that when they request funds to write off obsolete inventory, paralysis sets in. They can't get rid of the inventory because financial reserves don't exist to write off the inventory. The negative impact of an inventory write-off on the bottom line could mean missing profit expectations for the current quarter. However, in this case, the company fortunately was having a pretty good year; and some reserves were freed for the write-off. (One firm in our database routinely sets aside an amount every month for write-offs and eliminates a modest amount of obsolete inventory every month, never letting the problem grow too large.)

Manufacturing Flexibility

The working capital team members realized that their internal manufacturing operations were not flexible enough to react to demand changes. Manufacturing at this firm occurred in megafactories, each employing thousands of people. Production schedules were reset on a monthly basis and frozen, with long production runs being the norm. Two problems existed: (1) the thirty-day frozen period was much too long to stay in synch with demand changes, and (2) the long production runs meant that the company could only make twenty models in a typical day. Therefore, it took roughly a month to cycle through the five hundred SKUs made in a typical factory.

The team attacked the problem on both fronts, with a new process supported by new technology. The planning systems moved from monthly to weekly and eventually to daily cycles. Each major supplier was required to supply component parts with continually shorter lead times. And all this depended on a new mind-set that speed and flexibility were essential. This led to a range of initiatives using lean manufacturing concepts as the foundation to attack cycle times.

The firm successfully moved its manufacturing frozen period from thirty days to three weeks and then to two weeks. The frozen period was the time when the production schedule was locked in and could not react to changes in customer orders. At that point, it converted to a daily reduction goal, starting at a ten-working-day frozen period and targeting a reduction to five. Now, the planning systems could roll in a new refreshed schedule on the sixth day out, not thirty days. This breakthrough in flexibility allowed inventory to be reduced dramatically.

The team then attacked the issue of long production runs. Consistent with the lean manufacturing efforts, the number of SKUs that the factories could turn out each day doubled and then tripled. They accomplished this by aggressively reducing setup times and model changeover times on nearly every process, a very tedious and difficult undertaking. The manufacturing flexibility breakthroughs alone drove a major reduction in finished-goods inventory, because the company could now react to changes in demand with production flexibility, not simply inventory.

A number of manufacturing people initially resisted the changes. After all, they had to meet aggressive cost targets, and their intuition told them that more flexibility increases cost. But the COO took a personal interest in the initiative and embraced the need for more flexibility. He knew the future of the company and his bonus lay in serving the customers faster than the competition. He also suspected that by using lean concepts, more flexibility could be achieved with no additional cost. He strongly urged the manufacturing people to pursue flexibility. In the end, they found that more flexibility did not mean higher cost.

Inventory Segmentation

The team members decided they could not meet their goals and also carry the same amount of inventory across all models. They knew that many firms used a product segmentation system called ABC inventory classification. They decided to implement it and put some real teeth in it. They defined the A products as the fast movers, which were the top 50 percent of the models, generating 85 percent of the sales. Next, they defined the B products as the next 25 percent providing 10 percent of the sales. For these A and B products, the team changed very little. But they implemented a drastic change for the slow-moving C products—the remaining 25 percent of the models generating only 5 percent of the sales. For these low-volume products, the firm instituted a three-week lead time, so the products could be built to order and required no inventory. This totally eliminated the chronic problem of a highly disproportionate amount of inventory carried for these low-volume, slow-moving models by totally eliminating that inventory.

Initially, the sales function pushed back hard, concerned about a potential loss of market share. One sales manager said, "We might as well not even offer the C models for sale! We are going to lose a lot of sales to our competitors." The project was about to stall with this resistance. When the CEO heard of the problem, he passed the word down the organization that he was willing to take this risk and also in general wanted to see the functions collaborating with each other. (He had the right perspective. They were only risking 5 percent of the business.) So, finally, sales agreed to a test program with the concept piloted in one market first. The sales managers believed that the three-week lead time would result in lost sales and would clearly kill the initiative. On the contrary, the test market showed an actual increase in the overall business. When surveyed, retailers said that the sales increase was due to having better availability for the models that were selling.

Slow-Moving Inventory

The ABC inventory segmentation worked, but more effort was needed, since a lot of slow-moving and obsolete inventory still clogged the warehouses, some having been there for literally years. The working capital team agreed on a definition of slow-moving inventory as any inventory exceeding a thirty-day supply and was shocked to discover that nearly 30 percent of the inventory fell into that category. Reducing overall inventory was impossible without aggressive action on this front, then the other initiatives would deliver the results. The SKU reduction dovetailed with this initiative. The newly acquired manufacturing flexibility meant the firm could avoid long runs far in advance of actual demand. And ABC segmentation meant inventory on low-volume, impossible-to-forecast products could be kept very low.

Demand Managed to Equal Supply

One difficult problem remained that had to be addressed. Sales had little regard for manufacturing or supplier capability, and the supply people often ignored sales forecasts, which they felt were essentially fictional. The firm desperately needed a process to align supply with demand. It latched onto a process which many companies call sales and operations planning (S&OP). This cross-functional process involves sales, marketing, supply chain, manufacturing, finance, and so on in an activity to reach consensus on aligning supply with demand (we describe S&OP in much more detail in chapter 5). The company implemented both manager-level and executive alignment meetings to achieve full cross-functional buy-in. Although not perfect, the process provided an excellent forum in which to drive goal alignment and support the other cross-functional initiatives. At the end, sales had a demand plan and operations had a production plan that better aligned.

Finished-Goods Inventory Results

The four initiatives combined to drive nearly $250 million out of finished-goods inventory over the next three years. Product availability improved despite the inventory fall. As Taiichi Ohno, the father of lean manufacturing said, "The more inventory you have, the less you have of what you really need." This apparent contradiction holds true when inventory flows in sync with demand. The company learned it could dramatically lower inventory without hurting customer service by simply focusing its enhanced flexibility on models that were selling. The team was well on the way toward achieving its goal.

2. Raw and Work-in-Process Inventory

Even retailers and their suppliers could learn from the actions this manufacturer took to reduce its raw and work-in-process inventory. At the same time the finished-goods initiative proceeded, a subteam simultaneously attacked the raw material inventory in the factories.

This raw and work-in-process inventory (RWIP) was the entire inventory in the factories prior to becoming finished goods. RWIP consisted of inventory driven by a different set of factors than finished-goods inventory. Projects were launched in four areas with a stretch target to cut RWIP nearly 70 percent—to less than one-third of its starting level—eventually achieving a $75 million reduction over the next two years. The components of the plan were:

1. Reduce component part complexity. Fewer parts in the factories simplify processes and drive down cost.

2. Collaborate with the six hundred major suppliers to shrink component supply lead times, reduce costs, and improve quality.

3. Reduce the $40 million in nonproduction material such as maintenance supplies.

4. Continue implementing world-class (lean) manufacturing techniques.

The team discovered many egregious examples of component part complexity spinning out of control. For example, one product had thirty different types of wiring harnesses, with each harness consisting of fifteen to twenty-five wires. On two of those harnesses, everything was exactly the same except for one wire that was a quarter of an inch longer than the same wire on the other harness. Clearly, the design engineers had had no incentive to standardize parts, a situation that demanded a revision of engineering objectives to include factors other than minimizing component cost. With the right metrics in place, a significant reduction in component parts occurred over time.

The firm worked with each major supplier to set goals to reduce lead times. In return, all internal company forecasts were shared with the supply base. Nearly 30 percent of the components were converted to a vendor-managed inventory basis (VMI), with the suppliers now responsible for the inventory and for restocking until it was consumed.

Together, these projects reduced the days of inventory on hand from eighteen days of supply to less than five, which included the nonproduction material. This amounted to a $75 million inventory reduction over a two-year period.

3. Accounts Payable

The supply chain working capital team then ventured far from their traditional responsibilities and geared up to address accounts receivable and accounts payable. These nonfinancial people took awhile to fully understand the positive impact of payables on working capital. Like good and bad cholesterol, this was good working capital. The company had $300 million in payables and wanted to increase it to $450 million. How to increase payables was at first somewhat of a mystery to the team, but by collaborating externally with their suppliers, they found a way. Payment terms to suppliers were in the range of thirty to forty-five days. Finding a way to get as many suppliers as possible to ninety days became the objective. With ninety-day terms, the amount of payables doubled versus the old forty-five-day terms. The firm was able to hold on to its cash longer, reducing working capital.

This firm probably had enough clout with many of its suppliers to simply force them to increase payment terms. But the working capital team realized that in the long run it would be counterproductive. The team members wanted to find a win-win arrangement and worked with each core supplier to find a way to help offset the payment terms increase. This involved a combination of increased business for the core suppliers, longer-term contracts, and open sharing of data, technology, and strategy for the future. In addition, they developed an online information system, so suppliers could see when their invoice was scheduled for payment. This allowed suppliers to decide whether to wait for full payment or sell the invoice to a financial institution and receive payment the next day. Even better, they could generally sell the invoice based on their customer's investment grade credit rating. Over the next three years, the increase in payment terms resulted in a $150 million increase in accounts payable.

4. Accounts Receivable

The toughest area for the team members to address was accounts receivable. This $800 million gorilla was the largest component of working capital and could not be ignored if they were to meet the goal. Good progress in the other three areas meant that accounts receivable had to be cut "only" 20 percent or $175 million to make the overall working capital reduction goal of 50 percent. Could this possibly be done using supply chain tools? One common technique firms use to cut receivables is to simply sell them to a financial institution, a tactic called *factoring*. Anyone can factor receivables. But the working capital team asked, how can we cut them in reality? So the team focused now on collaborating externally at the other end of the chain, with its customers.

Receivables, of course, depend on payment terms. In a very real sense, negotiating payment terms with customers is the same thing as negotiating pricing, and that is normally led by the sales organization. Unfortunately, it's rare to find a company whose sales organization understands how to use the supply chain in these negotiations. Sales managers need either to involve the supply chain group in the customer negotiations or to fully understand the cost impact of agreeing to specific methods of storage and delivery. That's exactly what this team did.

The working capital team members decided to use faster resupply as a lever. As compensation for the benefit of faster resupply, the firm asked for a twenty-day reduction in payment terms from a base level of sixty days. This allowed them to reduce their accounts receivables by $95 million. Why would the customer agree to this change in payment terms? Because the firm showed its retail customer how it could greatly cut the inventory it was holding due to the much faster resupply. This was a win-win for both parties. The supplier reduced its working capital (accounts receivable), and so did the customer (inventory). Furthermore, the retail customer reduced its out-of-pocket costs for holding and storing the inventory.

Goal Achieved

In summary, the team members attained their goal and took $600 million out of working capital. They also slightly improved customer-order fill rates. Less inventory meant less inventory holding cost and also less need for warehouse capital. To drive this improvement with their supply chain, they used technology and collaborated externally with their suppliers and customers, and internally across the functional silos. And they had a disciplined process for managing change and getting things done. So, the team hit on all cylinders of economic profit. They greatly reduced invested capital, which indirectly cut cost, and contributed to revenue growth with the improved availability of product.

Speaking the Language of the
CEO and the Board

In the case described, the CEO patiently explained the concept and nuances of working capital to the supply chain executives. All supply chain leaders should ensure that they and their organizations understand the financial ratios critical to the executive team and the board, including ratios such as:

- Net profit margin (NOPAT) is net operating profit after tax.

- Capital turnover (CT/O) is revenue divided by total capital.

- Weighted average cost of capital (WACC).

- Return on invested capital (ROIC) is net profit margin multiplied by capital turnover (the same as net operating profit after tax divided by total capital).

- Economic profit (EP) is NOPAT less WACC.

Can the CEO help supply chain executives translate how their work drives NOPAT, CT/O, ROIC, and EP? If he does, he will unleash the power of the supply chain in a way not previously imagined. Supply chain executives have to know how their actions affect these ratios and drive economic profit for their firms. First, they need to improve their understanding of ratios, which may take some education and commonly available sources.[8]

Supply chain executives need to clearly understand why they must speak the language of the CEO and the board. The answer is the same one the famous bank robber Willie Sutton gave when asked why he robbed banks: "Because that's where the money is." It's a two-way street. If the supply chain organization wants the resources to make supply chain improvements, it needs to translate it into how it affects economic profit (see table 1-4).

TABLE 1-4

Supply chain terminology versus CEO and board terminology

CEO and board speak	Supply chain speak
NOPAT, CT/O, WACC, ROIC	Fill rate, shipments, and cost
COGS, SG&A	Transportation cost, warehousing cost
Working capital, cash flow, DSO	Inventory turnover
Shareholder value, PE ratio	Rarely mentioned
EBITDA	Cost, cost, cost
Economic profit	Rarely mentioned

Some companies such as OfficeMax have taken advantage of the opportunity to achieve supply chain excellence already and are using the language of the board to communicate about supply chain issues. (Reuben Slone, one of the authors, manages the supply chain at OfficeMax.) Every supply chain initiative at OfficeMax is evaluated based on its impact on economic profit. For example, the supply chain team doesn't just measure days of inventory, it measures the cost of days of inventory and thereby the impact on economic profit of decreasing days of inventory. Here's the calculation:

- Current inventory days: 55 days (6.5 turns per year)

- Inventory level: $1,068 million

- Investment per day of inventory held: $19.4 million

- Cost of capital: 8 percent

- Cost per day of inventory: $1.55 million[9]

The supply chain organization should look for simple forms of communication to make the work it does come alive for the CEO, the executive team, and the board. It needs to show the clear relationship between supply chain initiatives and shareholder returns. For more examples of how OfficeMax translates supply chain initiatives into economic profits, see table 1-5.

TABLE 1-5

How OfficeMax links economic profit and supply chain initiatives

Supply chain initiative	How each initiative is reframed into a driver of economic profit
Increased supply chain velocity	Lower inventory and lower working capital in general
More efficient use of physical assets like warehouses and scheduling of factories	Lower physical capital
Better availability and customer service	Higher sales
Lower distribution costs	Better margins

The executive team at OfficeMax realizes that the supply chain has a role in all of the components of economic profit and is a critical enabler to driving economic profit in all dimensions.

Conclusion

A small but growing number of companies are reporting that they leverage their supply chains to make working capital and cash flow improvements to drive economic profit and shareholder value. Supply chain organizations of the future must focus on far more than just driving out cost and improving product availability. Instead, they need to become engines of overall financial improvement for their companies. Smart companies will use innovation in their supply chain to generate the cash to fund further innovation in their product lines and growth in their business.

When the credit markets froze from 2008 to 2009, a few firms realized that they could free up cash internally without having to go to the bank. Huge amounts of cash exist. A study by AlixPartners showed that $562 billion is trapped in working capital across a thousand companies in fifty-six different U.S. industries.[10]

A major lesson learned in our work with many firms is that this focus must be driven from the top of the company. Without strong consistent support from the CEO, CFO, and COO, an initiative such as that described could not have been successful, due to the massive alignment of functional silos required. The fundamental learning from the case is how the supply chain can be used as a lever to dramatically lower working capital and improve cash flow. Since these changes positively affect economic profit, investors reward these efforts as they realize higher shareholder value.

The supply chain will not drive economic profit without a supply chain strategy. After working with hundreds of firms, we have found surprisingly few that have a real supply chain strategy.

The next chapter details how to develop such a strategy and the steps to take to build it. But there is a very basic prerequisite. The supply chain organization must challenge itself to take a broad, economic profit-based view, and must understand the CEO's language and that of the board.

ACTION STEPS

1. Translate supply chain actions into the language of the board and CEO.

2. Focus the supply chain strategy on driving economic profit and initiate supply chain projects that clearly drive the levers of economic profit. Openly communicate that strategy across the corporation.

3. Use the supply chain to not only attack cost and improve product availability, but also drive reductions in working capital on all fronts. Make the supply chain a cash flow creator and a driver of economic profit.

2

Supply Chain Strategy
and the Five Steps
to Achieving Excellence

A TOP-PERFORMING SUPPLY chain can be a powerful competitive weapon and an engine to drive economic profit. But without a road map, firms will fail to realize the full potential of supply chain excellence. Any effort to turn a supply chain that is simply functional into one that delivers significant value needs to start with a clear strategy. This may seem obvious. Yet in the supply chain audits we have done, very few firms could produce a supply chain strategy with a multiyear road map for achieving excellence. (Based on our data, less than 15 percent of firms have a documented supply chain strategy in place.) The self-test at the end of this chapter will help you determine where your firm stands.

What Is a Supply Chain Strategy?

A supply chain strategy starts with the same characteristics of any strategy, but includes the chain's unique challenges and characteristics. It is a road map that will guide the firm's supply chain evolution for the next three to five years.

A supply chain strategy absolutely must begin with the customers' current and future needs. It must comprehend the threats generated by foreign and domestic competition. It must recognize the most likely socioeconomic and demographic scenarios that may occur. It must honestly evaluate the strengths, weaknesses, opportunities, and threats (SWOT) the firm faces. The strategy must account for the evolving technology that is and will be available. It must satisfy the economic profit goals of the company. And, finally, it must generate a set of actions that create the capabilities the firm will need in the future. All pretty standard strategic planning stuff, so what's special about a supply chain strategy?

Seamless Flow of Products

Unlike other areas of the firm, the supply chain is a horizontal end-to-end process guiding the seamless flow of products across the extended enterprise. Products flow to customers from suppliers through the firm. But this flow must in effect pass smoothly through vertical functional barriers. In addition, the requirements of the customer must guide the flow, and those requirements must flow smoothly back through the functional barriers.

In other words, although products flow forward from suppliers through the firm to the customers, the strategic and information requirements should move backward, starting with the requirements of the customer, as illustrated in figure 2-1.

An effective strategy includes selecting the customers to serve, understanding what they value from the supply chain, planning

FIGURE 2-1

How material and information should flow across the extended supply chain

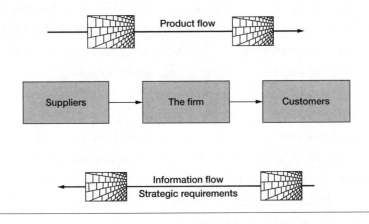

the products and services, and choosing the right supply chain partners in order to deliver that value.

Strategy, by its nature, goes beyond the quarterly and even the yearly time lines along which firms align their supply chain operations capacities. Transportation, inventory, facilities management, order management, and cash flow—these operational functions may reside within a shorter planning horizon, but they are critical to the fulfillment of any strategic plan. Likewise, without strategy, operations will be misdirected and ineffectual. Neither can stand alone. A strategic orientation has to be balanced with operational imperatives so that both are important, but neither overshadows the other.

Short-Term Thinking as a Barrier

In a recent supply chain forum survey we conducted, supply chain executives overwhelmingly said that short-term thinking in their companies was the greatest barrier to achieving supply

chain excellence. Following in lockstep from this short-term orientation are the quarter-end surges that plague many public
companies.

Consider how unnecessary quarterly variability disrupts the
flow of goods to the marketplace. In some cases, sluggish sales for
most of a quarter are capped by an end-of-quarter surge. In others,
goods move briskly for most of the quarter, only to slacken in
the final month. Both phenomena are caused by sales strategies
misaligned with supply chain planning objectives. This illogical
behavior manifests itself in many unintended ways. As one retailer
confessed, "I'm building two new warehouses to take advantage of
a supplier's end-of-quarter push." Quarter-end surges destroy economic profit, causing higher average inventories, higher costs, and
customer availability problems.

The Urge to Surge

Take the case of a large manufacturer of consumer products whose
quarterly demand from many retailers followed a three-month
sales pattern of low, low, high. In a meeting with the CEO, the
head of supply chain management pointed out the extreme costs
and supply disruptions for the disposable diapers product created
by a quarterly cycle consisting of overcapacity and inventory
buildup for two months, followed by rush production and delivery
in the third month.

The CEO doubted that anything could be done about it. After
all, wasn't that the natural demand pattern? Well, not exactly. The
supply chain leader diplomatically told the CEO that the underlying true demand was stable, and fluctuations were caused entirely
by his pushing the company to surge at the end of the quarter. By
accepting and managing to the quarterly sales numbers, the CEO
subtly signaled to retailers that, when the company was falling
short of its quarterly target, it would offer deep price discounts to
make the numbers. Thus, retail customers regularly bought a
three-month supply in the third month of each quarter so that

"low sales" by the company in the first two months of the next quarter would cause another discount surge.

As the CEO put it, "This was a real revelation for me. Babies pee at a constant rate, but our demand was fluctuating wildly. We trained our retail 'partners' to take advantage of us and order only in the third month of each quarter, when we were trying to make our numbers." The company subsequently offered consistent price and delivery terms each month, saving tens of millions of dollars in supply chain costs. (These costs had consisted of the combined impact of overtime during the surge, downtime and wasted labor during the slow sales months, and higher inventory costs in anticipation of the coming surge.) The company shared its savings in supply chain costs with the retail partners, effectively netting them better prices than they'd enjoyed under the old, high-cost, urge-to-surge supply chain game.

When companies surge at quarter end, inventory must be built up in advance to meet the spike. But because it's built early, it's often the wrong stuff. Product availability and fill rates take a hit, and much of the inventory remains in the warehouse, unsold, consuming cash, and destroying economic profit. The firm also must expedite product at a high cost in a mad rush to make the quarter end, sometimes monitoring shipments hourly. If that weren't bad enough, it inevitably spawns additional cost the following month, due to the resulting underutilized capacity.

Some executives tell us that stopping the quarter-end surge is next to impossible. They rightly point out that direct compensation is connected to bottom-line results; and total compensation is often tied to stock options and, therefore, share price. Given that stock price is often driven in the short run by quarterly results, it takes a lot of courage for the CEO and the board to move the company away from artificial end-of-quarter surges. The only chance of this happening is if the supply chain organization clearly demonstrates to the executive team that the practice over time creates more cost than benefit.

The Urge to Purge

Another manufacturer of consumer products exemplifies an additional, though rare, variation on the urge to surge: the urge to hold back. For example, demand from a company's retail customers followed a quarterly pattern of high, high, low. This triggered greater production capacity and expenses in the first two months, then inventory buildup during the third. Predictably, it also created operational disruptions for the company's suppliers. When the supply chain leader presented the problem to the CEO, they were both initially at a loss to explain this quarterly seasonal pattern, which seemed to affect all of the company's products. Like diapers, this company's products were staple items in grocery stores, and there was no logical explanation for the strange pattern in customer purchasing behavior. In fact, analysis showed that annual demand at the consumer level was fairly stable month to month.

So, why were retail customers ordering so illogically? After thinking it through, the supply chain leader realized that customers were actually forced into it by the company's salesforce, whose compensation program was structured to pay a commission that included a bonus for forecasting accuracy. The salesforce realized that its forecasts were used to set quotas. The CEO, whose background was in sales, wanted to motivate "rigor" in arriving at these de facto quotas. Motivation came in the form of commissions that were cut in half for any sales that exceeded the quarterly forecast. As the CEO had seen it, this would train salespeople to forecast accurately. If they set the forecast too high, they'd lose the bonus offered for forecasting accuracy; too low, and their commissions on higher sales would be halved.

Human nature being what it is, the salespeople were motivated to aim low and then stop selling once they'd hit their cautious marks. Company lore was that the salespeople were great forecasters. No doubt they appeared to be. For the first two months of each quarter, they sold diligently until they hit their quotas, after which they refused to take any further orders from retailers. Why take orders that would earn them only half the usual commission and cause them to lose their bonuses?

With this realization, the supply chain leader took every opportunity to highlight the negative impact of this practice on customer service, inventory, and supply chain costs. Customer surveys revealed that retailers' major complaint about the company was the difficulty (if not the impossibility) of obtaining its products at the end of a quarter. Consumers cited the inexplicable, cyclical lack of product availability. Because of the relentless persistence of the supply chain leader, the CEO finally realized that he was, in effect, paying his salesforce to disrupt its own supply chains and dissatisfy the customers, all to achieve the *illusion* of forecasting excellence. As with the urge to surge, these actions destroy economic profit by disrupting the normal flow of product, backing up inventory, depressing cash flow, and causing excess cost as the line operation reacts to rebalance capacity.

Antidote to Short-Term Thinking

A supply chain strategy encompassing five steps is the pathway to excellence and to economic profit. A good strategy begins by looking outside the firm at best practices across a wide industry range. However, many firms fail to challenge themselves with external best-practice benchmarking in the supply chain area. For example, a large pharmaceutical company was comfortable with annual inventory turns of about two, or six months of supply of inventory, yielding an average inventory of six months supply, even though its competitors were doing much better and were freeing hundreds of millions of dollars in cash by aggressively managing inventory and overall working capital.

Lack of best-practice benchmarking may not be the biggest problem. Many firms compound this inward focus by developing and reporting supply chain metrics that may actually conceal problems by neglecting crucial information. For instance, one construction-materials manufacturer reported "good availability" if inventory to fulfill a new order was simply somewhere in the system, regardless of whether the order was actually delivered to the customer on time. OfficeMax used to report a 96 percent weekly availability measure only at the product category level, thus not having a detailed view of the customer's experience from a store perspective. When Reuben Slone (one of the authors) took over as executive vice president of supply chain, he changed the metric to track product availability daily and by store location so that OfficeMax could measure (and manage) what the customer was experiencing. Now, even with this tougher, customer-focused measure, OfficeMax reports availability close to 99 percent.

Once a firm challenges itself with an external customer-oriented viewpoint and understands the best supply chain practices, it is ready to build its strategy using the five steps to supply chain excellence.

Five Steps to a Strategy for Supply Chain Excellence

We explained in chapter 1 that economic profit is the linchpin between shareholder value and supply chain excellence. But what truly generates supply chain excellence? Based on our ongoing analysis of hundreds of firms, five predominant elements clearly emerge as the components of supply chain excellence—and therefore five steps should form the basis for your supply chain excellence strategy. The remainder of this book lays out those steps along with specific actions to guide you in your journey. This chapter briefly introduces each step.

1. Pick the Right Leaders and Develop Supply Chain Talent

Finding and developing the right talent is the first step for a reason. Nothing is more important than having the right people with the right skills in the right jobs (see chapter 3). Yet, in researching this area, we have found some curious and alarming situations.

Skills Supply Chain Executives Need

Conversations with CEOs show that many fail to realize that the supply chain has become such a complicated set of activities—touching many business functions and processes, reaching beyond the enterprise, powered by fast-changing technologies, and presenting a range of strategic opportunities—that it can't be competently managed by the uninitiated, no matter how generally capable they might be. The supply chain discipline is at least as complex as any other, and senior supply chain executives should have education and/or significant experience in supply chain management. Yet we see plenty of examples of people without any supply chain background being made the chief supply chain executive. That makes as much sense as rotating someone from marketing into the comptroller or corporate treasurer position.

Flying Without a Talent Safety Net

At a major automotive components manufacturer, one of the very talented rising management stars was moved from marketing to lead the supply chain function. He was being groomed for a much larger role in the corporation, and this assignment was supposed to provide a key component in his development. At age forty-two, he could not afford any missteps at this point in his career. Unfortunately, shortly after he took over, an abrupt surge in demand for compact hybrid cars occurred, and his firm supplied a key, highly profitable component for the hybrids. Initially, there was no impact due to sufficient inventory in the system.

But, an experienced supply chain person would have immediately seen the looming problem of an impending stock-out and reacted very aggressively.

In this case, however, no appropriate action was taken for nearly two months, far too long to avert a major disruption in supply for the firm's automotive customers. With the stock-out nearly upon them, the carmaker turned to a backup supplier, permanently stopping purchases and transferring this extremely profitable business to another company. The new leader of the supply chain function found himself climbing a near-vertical learning curve in the midst of a major crisis, clearly a prescription for disaster. Within a year, the rising star, now severely tarnished, fell off the track to the top and moved to another area. The CEO learned from this experience and brought in a seasoned supply chain management expert from outside the company to set matters right. The new supply chain leader put in place an inventory management system, early warning systems, and inventory visibility tools to ensure that the firm never became paralyzed again.

2. Keep Up with Supply Chain Technologies and Trends

The second element of excellence is the rapid development of supply chain technology (chapter 4). It is useful to think of supply chain technology in four buckets (see examples in table 2-1).

Understand Available Technologies

Sophisticated technologies enable many of the most promising supply chain opportunities, so not only supply chain executives, but also the CEO and other senior executives should take the time to understand them at a high level. Supply chains are often densely complex. They entail cross-functional participation and deliver companywide benefits. They deeply permeate the firm and, as noted earlier, are most successful when they inspire the cooperation of external partners.

TABLE 2-1

Sample list of supply chain technologies

Supply chain technology category	Examples
Software	Forecasting systems
	Transportation management systems (TMS)
	Warehouse management systems (WMS)
	Distribution requirements planning (DRP)
	Inventory optimization software
	Network optimization and simulation software
	Production optimization software
	Collaboration software
	Enterprise resource planning (ERP) systems
	Customer relationship management (CRM) systems
e-business technologies	Automatic shipment notices (ASNs)
	Electronic data interchange (EDI)
	Electronic requisitioning
	Web-based data interchange and communication
	Electronic invoicing and payment, linked to shipments/receipts
	Exchanges/auctions
	Early warning and visibility systems
	Web 2.0 for collaboration
Visibility and productivity	Bar code
	Radio frequency data transmission
	Radio frequency identification (RFID)
	Pick to light
	Voice picking
	Automated picking
	Cellular/satellite tracking
	Carousel and conveyor systems
	Automated storage and retrieval systems (ASRS)
	Event management: visibility with real-time alerts
Process advances (apply these first)	Lean manufacturing
	Six sigma
	Vendor-managed replenishment (VMR)
	Collaborative planning, forecasting, and replenishment (CPFR)
	Activity-based costing
	Carbon footprint management

Major new software advances have enabled the optimization of distribution and production planning, inventory management, warehousing, and transportation systems. Assorted technologies such as radio frequency identification (RFID) tags, software used in ever more innovative ways, e-business tools, and other new technologies have emerged to support sophisticated supply chain management. Moreover, powerful process tools such as lean manufacturing to reduce cycle time and Six Sigma to reduce variability are being applied to the entire supply chain.

Most firms that have bought leading-edge supply chain systems acknowledge that they use only a fraction of the software's true capability and an even smaller fraction of the promised capability. An attentive senior executive can add weight and authority to the change management process, helping to drive user buy-in and make certain that proper vendor support, adequate training, and other resources are in place. Senior executives who understand new technologies serve a critical role by both motivating the organization to stay abreast of the rapidly changing technology landscape and asking the right questions to make sure the organization stays focused on the business case. In chapter 4, we lay out a framework for adopting new supply chain technology.

Moreover, senior executives who fully appreciate the challenges of deploying complex and costly systems can help their companies avoid classic missteps. The CEO of an industrial equipment manufacturer admitted to us that her company had experienced one such pitfall: "We spent $18 million getting an ERP package up and running in our company, and all we did was bring more modern technology to bear on supply chain processes that are forty years out of date. I expected this technology to bring supply chain costs down dramatically, and yet nothing changed. My mistake was expecting technology to solve a process challenge." She is now leading the company through a major effort to understand existing processes, identify opportunities to improve them, and adapt the new system to support the reengineered supply chain processes.

To excel in the technology area, senior executives should be briefed regularly about and have a high-level knowledge of supply chain technologies. They should also have a thorough understanding of how the firm applies these technologies and be capable of asking challenging questions—and recognizing the right answers— before any new technology is specified, purchased, and rolled out.

Huge Payback

When supply chain technology is successful, the payback is huge. A consumer packaged-goods manufacturer implemented an advance planning and scheduling (APS) system in 2002 that allowed it to make a significant advance in the way it managed its inventory. One major benefit was the ability to plan inventory safety stock for each SKU at each of forty-seven warehouse locations. This allowed the manufacturer to precisely target inventory to those SKUs in the specific cities where it was needed the most. Customer availability improved significantly, and over $200 million of inventory was removed. Was this all due to simply installing new software? Of course not, but the software standardized and automated the new *process* of managing inventory at the micro level, that is, for each SKU at each location.

That said, implementing APS modules is fraught with risk. One executive told us about an APS project that "completely blew up." In his company, the APS system not only determined production requirements for the factories, but also specified how to deploy the inventory in the warehouse network. Few decisions are more critical to a manufacturing company than these, and any mistakes are greatly magnified. Therefore such projects have a huge potential payback, but they do carry significant risk.

3. Eliminate Crippling Cross-Functional Disconnects

The third step toward supply chain excellence deals with the alignment of functions to support outstanding supply chain performance (see chapter 5). The supply chain process is the ultimate cross-functional process, stretching from suppliers through the entire firm and beyond to its customers. Yet in some firms, one wonders if the leadership team and even the CEO can explain the true role each function has in driving results across functional areas.

SKU management is a classic example of a cross-functional disconnect. Supply chain operating functions clearly feel the cost and the weight of inventory caused by more SKUs and their operational complexities. They also know that the more SKUs they offer, the more they will struggle to maintain product availability, as inventory is spread thinly across more SKUs. On the other hand, sales and marketing people feel just as strongly that they have to fight competition everywhere, and they absolutely must appear innovative to their customers, resulting in their strong motivation to increase product-line variety and complexity. Most firms struggle with this functional tension, often paralyzed into taking no action at all. All companies need the right number of SKUs to meet competition and foster innovation, but most have many more than necessary. Why can't they come to grips with this cross-functional dilemma?

A large manufacturer of consumer durables seemed to be way ahead of most companies. The CEO recognized the SKU problem after the supply chain leader brought him a compelling analysis showing the cost of the proliferating SKUs in the firm. He tasked the vice president of marketing with reducing SKUs by 20 percent. However, the marketing vice president believed that other objectives—growing market share, for example—were more important than the SKU goal, so he made no progress toward achieving it. As the vice president put it, "If I keep growing market share, my boss won't bother me about SKU count." Even though the CEO believed strongly in SKU reduction (it had paid big dividends at his former company), he lacked the knowledge to make it an equally urgent objective for the vice president.

In part, this was because the CEO didn't understand supply chain operations well enough to know *why* it had paid off for his former company. That deficit compromised his ability to persuade the vice president of his seriousness.

Inventory is another cross-functional sinkhole. In company after company, the sales organization will not use markdowns to move obsolete inventory, because the sales metrics exclude the costs of carrying that inventory. The firm then pays both the carrying costs and—sometimes years later—the cost of the inevitable markdown. This destroys economic profit on two fronts. Inventory grows and depresses cash flow, and margins inevitably decline when the firm finally confronts the issue.

To avoid such needless inefficiencies, the company's senior leaders should be personally involved in a mature sales and operations planning process (described in chapter 5). SKU complexity should be tracked and decreasing, as should obsolete inventory. Operations, supply chain, sales, and marketing should be held equally accountable for customer service and inventory. Supply chain leaders must help the CEO thoroughly understand,— so that he or she can help to harmonize the interplay of cross-functional and supply chain priorities. A smooth-flowing horizontal process from suppliers to customers cannot be managed effectively with vertical functional silos blocking the way.

The Right Incentives and Metrics

What is measured gets rewarded and what is rewarded gets done. Consider a major North American railroad's struggle with this concept. Although the railroad's most profitable customers were well-known within the firm, terminal managers, who were measured on how many railcars they moved with the available locomotives, did not reflect this knowledge operationally. The performance metric motivated terminal managers to assign priority status to longer trains, even though that might leave the shipments of high-value customers languishing for days in the terminal. In one case, goods shipped by a $100 million customer regularly missed delivery dead-lines because locomotives were consistently diverted to trains loaded with marginally profitable goods that didn't require expedited shipment but got it nonetheless.

Alignment of Metrics

Any new strategy requires new ways of working, and metrics must support those new behaviors. No behavior is more important to supply chain excellence than all functions pulling together in unison to drive economic profit by serving the customer flawlessly with the lowest possible cost and asset investment. When metrics are accurate and functionally aligned, magic can happen. In 1998, when Paul Dittmann (one of the authors) was at Whirlpool, the company put in place a set of metrics to track the effectiveness of all functions and, especially, the supply chain, in attacking working capital. As a result, the company cut working-capital day's sales outstanding (DSO) in half and became the leader in the appliance industry. Once a good set of aligned metrics supporting the strategy is in place, senior executives should establish reward and incentive programs to encourage employees to behave in ways that benefit the overall firm, not just their own functions.

For example, the CEO and sole owner of a grocery products manufacturer led the organization through an extensive analysis of its supply chain processes. The result was an ambitious strategic plan to take advantage of supply chain management across the firm and with its partners. The goal—to save the company an estimated $3 million a year—directly targeted the bottom line. The biggest challenge to the strategic plan was that it would require major changes in how the manufacturer managed various aspects of its internal operations. The strategic planning process culminated when the CEO met with the executive team to review the plan's rollout over a two-year horizon. In the middle of this meeting, he paused to observe, "You're talking about putting $3 million a year in my pocket, and it's just occurred to me that

I'm the only one in the room excited about it." On the spot, he pledged to create a special annual million-dollar bonus pool above and beyond the company's normal bonus system. Any employee who could demonstrate having a significant role in the success of the supply chain plan would get a portion of the pool. The CEO defined success as achieving the $3 million bottom-line improvement.

"Any year in which that happens, the special bonus pool exists," he said. He then instructed his three direct reports to devise a metric-and-compensation system (which he would personally review) for measuring individuals' contributions to the success of the plan and to determine how bonuses should be paid out. Suddenly, everyone in the company became a supply chain enthusiast.

The owner of this company was a very clever man. How do you make certain you can clear a $3 million hurdle? You aim to be far above it. In the first year of implementing the supply chain reform plan and its special bonus, the bottom line improved not by $3 million, but $3.75 million. Employees were so intent on achieving the $3 million goal that they actually overachieved, in effect paying for three-fourths of their own bonuses.

4. Collaborate with Suppliers and Customers

The fourth step toward supply chain excellence requires the ability to collaborate externally with suppliers and customers (see chapter 6). To build the seamless flow of products to the customer and the seamless flow of information back from the customer, collaboration must extend outside the walls of the firm. The grocery products manufacturer in our earlier example had six key suppliers and three key retailers to collaborate with. At the supply chain leader's urging, the CEO met personally with the CEOs of each supplier, explained the strategy thoroughly, and pledged that for any year in which a supplier fully cooperated and the improvement goal was achieved, the company would not press the supplier for price cuts. Moreover, any savings to the company directly attributable to the supplier's efforts would be shared fifty-fifty. In essence, the company was now paying the suppliers to help it make its supply chain strategy work. The company made similar arrangements with the retailers. As a result, the manufacturer had a supply chain with six key suppliers and three key retailers all working in concert—and were rewarded for doing so—to make the strategic plan succeed. Not surprisingly, it did.

Chapter 6 details the best practices in collaborating externally and illustrates them with several case studies, laying out a pathway for success. Unfortunately, the barrier often lies within the firm itself. Supply chain considerations (and expertise) should be core components of business planning—including sales and marketing promotions—and of contract negotiations with customers and partners. Customers and suppliers should be prioritized and dealt with accordingly. If you can't prioritize your customers, you don't stand a chance at developing a successful collaboration. Once priorities are established, it is possible to achieve breakthrough results by collaborating with the core, critically important suppliers and customers.

5. Implement a Disciplined Process of Project and Change Management

The fifth and last step toward supply chain excellence is arguably the most critical. Without a disciplined process to get things done, everything else becomes irrelevant (see chapter 7). Senior executives must set the tone for managing change. Senior management must have the discipline to constantly communicate a simple clear message, over and over.

Supply chain projects consistently consume the most IT resources in firms, and the supply chain organization constantly tackles projects that are highly cross-functional and cross-company in nature. The requirement for excellence in project management practices must start in the CEO's office and with the executive team in order to ensure that these tough cross-functional supply chain projects are successful. The CEO must demand that the project teams work on the root causes, not just the symptoms. She must encourage them to manage project scope carefully to keep complex supply chain projects manageable. She must constantly urge them to stay focused on the benefits and business case. She must make sure that project teams have identified risks and have a mitigation plan. And finally, knowing that people issues are her biggest implementation risk, she must require that all major initiatives have a change management plan for both implementing and sustaining change.

A culture of project success starts at the top of the firm. Once started, getting things done in the cross-functional, cross-company supply chain requires a disciplined process of project management and change management. Chapter 7 lays out the biggest risks to supply chain initiatives and the best practices for getting them done.

Conclusion

In summary, supply chain excellence flows from a supply chain strategy built on the five elements of supply chain excellence (see figure 2-2).

The next chapters discuss each of these five steps. Chapter 8 contains two case studies that show how a supply chain strategy achieved by the steps toward excellence can drive economic profit and shareholder value.

Evaluation Test for Senior Executives

Do the average CEO, board member, and senior executives understand the five steps toward supply chain excellence? This evaluation tool measures the quality and depth of senior executive

FIGURE 2-2

Supply chain excellence flows from a strategy built on the five elements of supply chain excellence

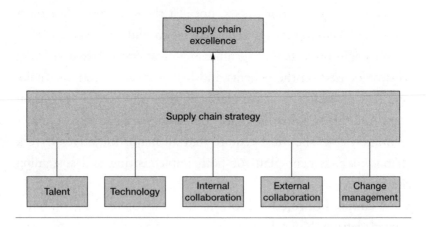

involvement in supply chain strategy by assessing the programs that have—and haven't—been put in place. It further shows the sobering degree of challenge supply chain leaders face in educating the company. A scoring guide is included with the tool.

A poor score means you should take action quickly:

Start by hiring the best supply chain professionals available.

Get personally involved in cross-functional issues like S&OP, complexity management, and working-capital management.

Gradually lead the company away from quarter-end disruptions, even though extremely difficult.

Reward supply chain behavior that benefits the entire company.

Invest personal time in learning more about recent advances in the supply chain field, including the profusion of new technologies.

Use benchmarking and leverage outside experts.

A good score on the evaluation doesn't mean there's time to waste gloating, but instead offers the opportunity to build aggressively on the company's supply chain strengths and drive the organization to increasing its advantage over the competition.

Evaluate Your Level of Supply Chain Leadership

Answer the six questions in the left-hand column in table 2-2. Assign a score from 1 to 9, according to your current level of supply chain leadership. The statements within each column will help you decide where you fall on the leadership spectrum. A scoring guide appears in table 2-3.

How Do Senior Executives Score on This Test?

At a recent University of Tennessee supply chain forum, thirty-five companies participated in the evaluation. The distribution of scores is shown in figure 2-3.

These firms ran the gamut in size and type from $100 million in sales to $95 billion. They included manufacturers, retailers, and service providers across a wide industry spectrum. A participant from each company took the test and answered as he or she thought his or her CEO would answer. Table 2-3 shows how the companies score in general versus the standards outlined.

Which Areas Are the Greatest Problem?

Which supply chain area ranked as the worst problem when evaluating the data? All of them are major problem issues, but some are worse than others. The supply chain categories listed problems from *least problematic to worst* according to the average score received:

Supply chain valued as a career in the firm

Supply chain technology reasonably understood

TABLE 2-2

Test for the Senior Executives. See scoring guide below in Table 2-3.

Question	Score								
	1	2	3	4	5	6	7	8	9
1. Do you have a supply chain strategy supported with the right metrics and incentives?	No supply chain strategy exists in your company.			A strategy document exists, but you cannot summarize all of the key elements of the plan.			A full supply chain strategy exists that your organization buys into, and it is supported with good metrics and incentives.		
2. Is supply chain a valued career path in your company?	You do not need to get involved in career planning for supply chain personnel. You do not understand why your supply chain leader must have a supply chain background.			You are establishing a plan to develop or enhance supply chain talent in your company. You see the major impact of supply chain on the firm's success.			You chose an experienced supply chain professional to lead the supply chain organization. You are involved in the hiring of key supply chain personnel.		
3. Do you collaborate externally with your suppliers and customers?	Customer-focused metrics are not in place, nor are supplier scorecards. You do not formally prioritize your suppliers and customers. You do not know whether supply chain partners have been enlisted to support your supply chain goals.			Some suppliers and customer metrics are in place and efforts are in place to make them more realistic and credible. You have some effort underway to share data and strategies with your suppliers and customers. Some effort at mutual improvement projects exists.			Data and strategies are fully shared with your key suppliers and customers. You have mutual win-win improvement projects underway, and some have been successfully implemented.		

4. Are your internal functions aligned?	You are not involved in function leaders' formulation of incentives and goals to make sure they are aligned and support the supply chain.	You have some understanding of how compensation, bonus, and commission programs might inadvertently harm supply chain and profit performance.	You actively support efforts to reward employees, suppliers, and customers that contribute to your supply chain efficiency.
5. Do you understand important supply chain technologies and trends?	You have little interest in new supply chain technologies and leave that to the experts.	You periodically become aware of—and are curious about—advances in supply chain technology.	You have a good knowledge of supply chain technologies and of plans to apply them in your firm. You feel you know the right challenging questions to ask about supply chain technologies.
6. Do you have a disciplined process for getting things done?	There are no formal project and change management processes in place.	A project and change management process exists, but implementation results are mixed.	You demand that disciplined project and change management processes are in place, evidenced by consistent implementation success.

FIGURE 2-3

Distribution of scores from test for 35 companies

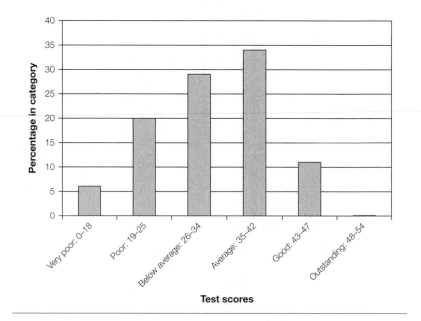

Test scores

TABLE 2-3

Scores of senior executives from 35 companies

A score of 4 or lower on any question is a yellow flag. An immediate remediation effort is in order in that area.	61% of companies
A total score of 21 or lower is a red flag to any manufacturing, distribution, or retail senior executive; the lack of supply chain focus may be fatal.	Occurred in 2 of the 35 companies
With a total score in the 22–42 range, recovery is possible if the suggestions are followed.	94 percent of companies scored in this range
With a total score of 43 to 54 points, the supply chain can be a true competitive advantage.	None of the 35 companies scored in this category

Collaboration with suppliers and *customers*

A disciplined process for getting things done

Cross-functional alignment adequate

Lack of a supply chain strategy; short-term thinking dominates decision making

A short-term focus on decision making seems to be the greatest disease plaguing supply chain effectiveness, closely followed by cross-functional misalignment. Clearly, the company's senior executives, with the coordinating support of the supply chain leader, need to play the key role in attacking these two barriers to excellence. On the positive side, it is good to see the emergence of supply chain's value as a career path.

ACTION STEPS

1. Develop a supply chain strategy based on the five steps and support it with the proper set of metrics and incentives.

2. Pick the right leader for the supply chain organization (chapter 3).

3. Keep up with supply chain technology and trends (chapter 4).

4. Eliminate cross-functional disconnects that cripple the supply chain (chapter 5).

5. Collaborate with suppliers and customers (chapter 6).

6. Implement a disciplined process of project and change management to successfully get things done (chapter 7).

3

Hiring the Right Talent

THE FIRST STEP TOWARD the strategy to drive supply chain excellence is assembling the right talent. If you don't have the right people in place you can't build an appropriate strategy and you certainly can't execute it. Finding talent for supply chain positions has unique challenges due largely to the cross-functional and cross-company process challenges that supply chain executives face.

Unique Skills Needed

In several conversations with executives of multibillion dollar firms in 2007 and 2008, we found a surprising lack of understanding of the true nature of the modern supply chain process. In some cases, a number of those we interviewed defined the supply chain extremely narrowly as simply the process of dealing with the firm's suppliers. Unfortunately, many firms still live with just such an outmoded view.

Ten years ago, the supply chain leader in most companies held a title such as vice president of logistics. It was a largely functional role that relied on technical proficiency in discrete areas: knowledge of shipping routes, familiarity with warehousing equipment and distribution-center locations and footprints, and a solid grasp of freight rates and fuel costs. He reported to the COO or CFO, had few prospects of advancing further, and had no exposure to the executive committee. The way companies need to think of the modern supply chain executive has changed dramatically.

Beyond Functional Expertise

Supply chain executives still need to be experts at managing supply chain *functions* such as transportation, warehousing, inventory management, and production planning. But the supply chain *process* extends end to end and even outside the firm, including the relationships with suppliers and customers on a global basis. Leading firms now see the supply chain functional leader as the necessary executive to coordinate the end-to-end supply chain process, even though he or she does not control it all. Because of that added dimension of cross-function, cross-company coordination, senior supply chain executives must possess a number of unique characteristics, which we describe in detail next. In our interactions, we find that many firms have not yet come to that realization. In a *Supply Chain Management Review* study, 60 percent of companies still do not have an executive officer who manages even the normal set of supply chain functions.[1] Further, in our experience, of the 40 percent that do have such a position, the vast majority still have not tasked that executive with full authority to coordinate the end-to-end process.

The CEO in particular should understand that the battle for top supply chain talent must be focused on acquiring people with *process* expertise, not simply *functional* competence. The mental shift to the supply chain as a process leads inevitably to a shift in the role of the supply chain executive from a functional focus to a process focus, and to supply chain becoming part of the executive team.

Part of the Executive Team

In a growing but still small number of firms, the supply chain chiefs of high-performance companies don't just have access to the executive team, they're part of it. That role requires bringing value in not only educating the CEO and the board and giving them the vocabulary to talk about the supply chain and its critical role in creating economic profit, but in finding and driving opportunities to increase economic profit. The job in those progressive firms is no longer a mostly functional one, but instead plays a key strategic role that can influence 60 percent to 70 percent of a company's total costs, all of its inventory, and most aspects of customer service.

The supply chain leader in these progressive firms has global responsibility for coordinating processes across functional silos like sales, R&D, and finance, as well as functional responsibility for activities like procurement, logistics and production planning, and customer service. He or she pays as much attention to the demand side as to production and materials planning, and knows what it takes to reliably deliver products to customers and build mechanisms to learn what customers have to say. In some firms, the role of the senior supply chain executive expands so much that he or she essentially becomes the COO, especially in those companies where the COO does not traditionally have responsibility for sales, marketing, or merchandising.

In this transformed world, even CEOs who previously had little contact with the supply chain leader must now demonstrate supply chain expertise. Indeed, supply chain chiefs have even become viable candidates for CEO succession. Walmart's past CEO Lee Scott, who previously headed transportation, distribution, and then logistics for the retailer, is just one example. Michael Duke, his successor, also has a big dose of supply chain experience in his background. "The supply chain has elevated itself to one of the major items on an enterprise risk spectrum that is discussed at even audit committees and board of director meetings," said Mayo A. Shattuck III, chairman, president, and CEO of Constellation Energy Group. "The CEO really has to be a supply chain expert and cannot just delegate that completely to someone else."[2] And it's up to the company's supply chain professionals to find ways to educate the CEO. For example, one supply chain leader told us that after much badgering, he talked his boss, the executive vice president of operations, into scheduling a monthly supply chain update with the CEO. Now after eight months of those reviews, he says that the CEO clearly understands it at a much deeper level and now mentions supply chain advances in most of his public comments.

However, the majority of firms fall far short of this ideal. Many companies don't have a complete end-to-end process view of their supply chain and face a big problem if their competitors get it before they do. But, "getting it" isn't enough. They also have to win the battle for supply chain talent.

The Battle for Supply Chain Talent

Supply chain executives who are keen to upgrade the caliber of their leadership quickly find that demand for top talent outweighs supply, regardless of the economic circumstances. This executive staffing challenge is exacerbated by the fact that seasoned supply chain experts are aging, and more firms are gradually expanding the role of their supply chain leaders. Therefore, demand has exploded, with insufficient high-potential candidates coming up to fill the needs. Further compounding the issue, top candidates are well aware of their options and are very selective in what they choose to do and where they choose to do it. Acquiring top talent is particularly difficult in regions where supply chains are expanding the most, as countries like India and China have yet to develop a rich pool of executives with international experience and supply chain expertise. But to remain competitive, organizations have to expand their search for talent globally.

While CEOs may now have higher expectations of supply chain management, many are still unclear about just which qualities the candidates need to succeed. Only a CEO who is current with supply chain practices and trends can properly evaluate a supply chain executive's performance. Given the importance, CEOs need to clearly understand the critical characteristics of top supply chain talent, and as indicated earlier, it is incumbent on senior supply chain managers to educate the CEO.

Critical Characteristics of Top Supply Chain Talent

A company can acquire the best talent only after identifying it. To select the right people to oversee the increasingly pivotal supply chain responsibility, CEOs must know the blueprint for the ideal supply chain leader. These characteristics can be grouped into five key qualities:

- Global orientation

- Systems thinking

- Inspiring and influential leadership

- Technical savvy

- Superior business skills

Supply chain executives don't have a monopoly on these characteristics. Any senior executive must possess the same skills. But there are some unique needs in the supply chain area that arguably make them even more essential. As an executive said in one of the supply chain audits we do for firms, "We must find a way to avoid a functional food fight, and align for the good of our customers." As stated earlier, supply chain executives have normal functional responsibilities just like other senior executives, but far more than others, they need to coordinate areas outside their direct control as well as activities of suppliers and customers on a global basis. This is a skill well outside many traditional executive team members' experience and illustrates just one of the nontraditional capabilities required to achieve supply chain excellence.

Global Orientation

Of course, nearly all senior business executives need to be globally savvy. Global sourcing and supply chains have expanded tremendously in recent years, for both retailers and manufacturers. There are few companies that do not either source globally, sell globally, or have competitors that do. Therefore, supply chain executives must manage an enterprise that extends across continents and must deal effectively with suppliers and customers worldwide.

Global Risk

Five years ago, a manufacturer of telephone equipment decided to transfer all its manufacturing and sourcing from the Midwestern United States to Asia, mainly China. Suddenly, the firm's leaders found that its supply chain staff needed skills that were very different. They found communications with their new Chinese suppliers to be a difficult issue. For example, they scheduled meeting after meeting to discuss the problem with the one-hundred-ten-day lead times. (The firm should have known about this lead-time problem in advance, but incorrectly and naively assumed lead time would be transit time plus a couple of weeks, or forty-five days.) At the end of each meeting, the supplier agreed to address the problem, but month after month nothing happened. They bluntly asked the Chinese supplier if it understood the need to shorten lead times and they always heard yes. But later, they discovered that yes did not really mean yes; instead it meant, "We heard you, and we want to avoid an argument."

This firm was suddenly facing a very different culture and had to deal with a vastly expanded supply chain. The leaders scrambled to bring in people with global experience from outside the company and realized that they needed to develop more global expertise internally. Embroiled in this crisis, they asked several key people to pack up their families, move to South China, and undergo a very difficult expatriate assignment. Meanwhile, customer service suffered, with dire results. When a shift in demand for the firm's products occurred, it was a hundred ten days from reacting to the change, causing it to lose sales and nearly a quarter of its market share to its main competitor.

Cultural Differences

Managing an international supply chain function requires far more than knowing what time it is in Shenzhen or what the proper meeting etiquette is in Dubai. Increasingly, it calls for the basic ability to function effectively in other cultures. Global executives need deep, fact-based, problem-solving skills. They need to focus more on forging relationships, which are far more important in most countries than in the United States. They need to understand that activities in a global environment take longer and plan their projects accordingly.

In international corporations, building a team requires that multiple nationalities and cultures be combined and somehow integrated into the corporate culture. Jay Fortenberry, vice president of logistics and planning at Honeywell, says, "Sure, we need to find the right technical skills, but the real challenge is assembling a global team with the right chemistry that can effectively work together, and that must be done at the point of hiring." Once the team is assembled, the fun is just beginning. Language is always a challenge, but almost everyone speaks some form of English. In addition, executives face a plethora of daily issues that many are not prepared for.

For example, there is never a good time for a staff meeting. One young executive stationed in Singapore with a U.S.-based consumer packaged-goods company said he was expected to be on conference calls nearly every night from approximately 8 p.m. to midnight and that the headquarters crowd always spent the first fifteen minutes making jokes that those on the phone couldn't hear or understand. Clearly, companies need a firm discipline policy for conducting global conference calls.

Laws and customs can also be extremely confusing. An executive from a manufacturing company told how he had to plan around the long paternity leaves in Europe. He also found that although furloughs may work well in the United States as a quick cost-cutting move, they are not so easy to implement in other countries, which have severe restrictions on layoffs. One young expat told us that in the United States, people tend to talk of an "Asian" culture. But, as he said, "There's a big difference for me in dealing with a manager from the Philippines versus one from Japan." A Latin American manager from a very large *Fortune* 10 company explained a similar situation, "Even though we speak a common language, Spanish (except for Brazil), there are so many differences from one country to the next that it's easy to get lost in translation. Even as a regional Latin American manager, I find it very challenging to clearly understand the different meanings of a message in different Latin American countries."

Young people are extremely ambitious everywhere, but in some countries in Asia, the expectation is that they will make a career move at least every two years. What motivates someone in one culture may not work in another. Compensation packages in some cultures may need to emphasize noncash rewards such as an emphasis on enhancing a worker's reputation in the community. Ethics and laws differ widely. One executive told us that he was shocked to learn that some companies in Europe share transportation rate quotes with competitors to try to get a lower cost, something that would never happen in the United States.

Finally, global executives learn quickly that they must travel, even in this age of electronic communication. Personal relationships are far more critical outside the United States. As Fortenberry says, "Good leaders recognize the value of face-to-face interaction with people in other cultures. We cannot rely on e-mail to have productive relationships." However, this will evolve gradually over time. For example, the next generation of video conferencing will have a significant impact. The new high-definition video conferencing, with transmissions in real time and without the infuriating delays, will help reduce some but never all of the need for global travel.

Executives we've talked with say that resources to help them learn about global differences are few and far between. Just being aware of the myriad rules and regulations is a daunting task. Most have learned via experience, which may be the only effective way to truly internalize global knowledge. It's why companies like P&G require their high-potential employees to have a global assignment before promoting them to the executive level. And it's why supply chain executives with global knowledge are so extremely valuable.

Managing Expats

Many top supply chain executives have worked abroad, most for several years. With components, subassemblies, and finished goods coming from China, Thailand, India, Mexico, and beyond, along with a global marketplace, companies need supply chain management executives who can manage complexities beyond traditional borders. Nothing prepares them better than an expatriate assignment.

Supply chain executives who have worked in other countries truly understand the global environment and are extremely valuable. An expat employee working for a consumer products company told us, "We have been through the fire of being treated as temporary employees that try to execute radical, strategic change. We have faced the huge challenge of integrating our families into a totally new culture, along with the confusion surrounding visa restrictions, spouse jobs, taxes, and so on, as well as the equal challenge of reentry after the expat assignment is completed. And we also know that we need to somehow stay visible in the home location so we won't be forgotten for career planning." People who have been through this expat experience can guide their firms through the global environment.

Systems Thinker

Unlike some other senior executives, supply chain executives must embrace the added dimension of cross-functional and cross-company complexity—the challenge that comes with thinking of the supply chain as a system. Manufacturing or sales executives must develop deep expertise and a strategy for their areas. But the supply chain executive must also comprehend the connections and interdependencies across procurement, logistics, manufacturing, and marketing or sales. In addition, he or she must also absorb the complexity of interfaces outside the firm with suppliers and customers. As one supply chain executive put it, "We are the discipline that attempts to integrate multiple functional competencies both inside and outside the firm into a comprehensive, interconnected system. It seems like we supply chain people run a systems optimization problem every day, with the inputs constantly changing."

Systems thinkers have strong analytical skills. For example, as they plan a risk-mitigation strategy to anticipate tighter customs regulations at a foreign port, or as they develop a precise understanding of how a customer's upcoming seasonal promotion will require new shipping options, they need to be skilled at rigorous analysis of a wide range of data input, followed by clear decisions that are backed by contingency plans.

After completing the analysis, the best supply chain executives are also masters of change management. Not only do they envision the entire organization in constant flux, but they know how to manage the moving components that make up the entire chain, from distant suppliers to the end customer to the internal functions in the company. One supply chain executive told us, "By understanding the key performance measures of my sales counterpart, I was able to show her how it was in her best interest to increase the minimum number of units we should require customers to order. When she made that change, we were able to fill trucks faster, and get out the loads to the customers on time."

A world where supply chains stretch to thousands of miles and customers become more fickle requires multiple perspectives. Low-cost manufacturing may not lead to lower total costs if time-to-market factors are considered. Every decision must be weighed not by how it affects one aspect of the supply chain, but by its impact on end-to-end performance.

Hau Lee of Stanford University points to a need for a broad systems view, particularly in emerging economies. When supply chain managers ask for Lee's advice on China, they frequently emphasize labor-cost comparisons only, when they should be looking at the total landed cost of their global supply chains, including not only labor, material, and freight costs, but also inventory cost and even the risk-adjusted cost to the business of potential disruptions.[3]

Focused on more than just cost reduction, the best supply chain experts start with the perspective of the customer. This calls for a firm grasp of what the customer values, a full understanding of the big reasons why the company is on its customers' preferred supplier lists, and a collaborative relationship that encourages customers to share their future plans. Armed with this input, supply chain leaders are able to view their activities as sources of competitive advantage.

Systems thinkers interact directly face to face with their company's customers, because they know that the customer is the one immutable anchor of an extremely complex system. They do the same with their suppliers. Systems thinkers also take planned but not wild risks to avoid unforeseen consequences. They try to mitigate the risks that exist. For example, on the procurement side, the risks of having too much product in the wrong place at the wrong time can be alleviated by product modularity and proved postponement strategies. A world of ever longer supply chains multiplies opportunities for things to go wrong and demands creators of well-constructed contingency plans focused on flexibility and resilience.

Supply chain systems are so complex that there are often unforeseen consequences. For example, a CEO's dictate to expand global product outsourcing in order to reduce cost may instead lead to unforeseen increases in inventory and perhaps even a catastrophic supply failure. This is exactly what happened to one apparel manufacturer. Two years after outsourcing a major portion of its product line to Asia, it decided to do a complete analysis, since it simply was not seeing the result on the bottom line. It was aghast to find that the real cost savings from an outsourcing initiative totally disappeared when inventory costs, exchange rate fluctuations and hedging, and lost sales (due to supply disruptions) were factored into the analysis.

Inspiring and Influential Leadership

A small but growing number of supply chain leaders are at the front and center of the organization. They foster close interpersonal relationships that build credibility for themselves and for the function across the organization. They build teams and manage people and communicate their message compellingly to multiple stakeholders. They are influencing others in the firm to work together to create a world-class supply chain. They are masters at building close collaborative relationships with their companies' leaders in sales and marketing, human resources, and finance. As twenty-year veteran senior executive coach Vicky Gordon explains, "Inspiring leaders are passionate about all aspects of the business. They must be able to engage people's heads and hearts to make difficult decisions that are in the best interests of the entire business not just one function. They are not just great technical experts."[4]

Chinese philosopher Lao Tzu once wrote, "Of the best leaders, when their task is accomplished, their work done, the people all remark, 'We have done it ourselves.' "[5] In the same way, all the disparate functions in the firm must embrace a common supply chain direction as their own. This does not happen without an uncommon ability to influence the organization beyond areas of direct control. Backing up the inspirational approach is clear communication of the firm's vision and mission and constant recognition and promotion of teamwork.

Effective communication is all the more critical when supply chain teams extend across nations, requiring leaders to influence people who don't report to them. This is clearly a challenge that some supply chain leaders have yet to meet. In a global survey of supply chain progress, only 35 percent of respondents agreed or strongly agreed that their supply chain strategies and goals are communicated to all employees.[6] Nearly half indicated that there is little or no alignment between the supply chain function and their company's business strategy.

Gordon believes that the skills needed by supply chain leaders to be effective and influential communicators have also changed due to the expansion of their global responsibilities: "The immediacy—the speed at which we work and live has fundamentally changed the communication process for leaders. In the past if you could give a good speech, of course with Power-Point slides, and could lead a meeting successfully, that was considered adequate communication abilities for leaders. Today leaders must be able to communicate through many channels and mediums in real time. To do this a leader must have improvisational skills to be able to quickly adapt messages to audiences around the world, in different cultures, and across generations."[7]

To be effective, supply chain leaders, perhaps even more than other executives, have to move from an "I sent the e-mail, we held the meeting" approach to communicating in a collaborative way. In this model, listening is a more important skill than speaking. A good supply chain communicator will understand the motivations of his counterparts in other functions, gather feedback and concerns from areas like sales and marketing, and communicate in their language how the issues are being addressed.

Inspirational supply chain leaders ensure that everyone throughout the organization understands and is committed to supply chain excellence. One way they do this is through the highly adept development of the leaders below and behind them. This is particularly important since supply chain leaders are, to a certain extent, corporate trailblazers. Supply chain management as a stand-alone practice is relatively new. Previously, purchasing fell under the CFO, warehousing under operations, and vendor relations under purchasing and marketing, with only logistics sometimes its own function.

Supply chain leaders with their wide-reaching global responsibilities need to coach younger managers to know the company inside and out, well beyond their own areas of responsibility. They should encourage young talent to constantly search for new processes and practices, since those who don't understand the world beyond their manufacturing or distribution area will find it difficult to become more than effective managers of a process.

Developing a talent pipeline of inspiring supply chain leaders is not easy. There are three systemic obstacles senior executives typically encounter that block such development. Given that top supply chain talent is in especially short supply, the following problems, elaborated by David Wright, CEO of Verari Systems, Inc., particularly affect development of supply chain talent: "First, most companies only reward bottom-line results such as profits or sales. Growing human capital to achieve results is typically neither measured nor rewarded. Second, the responsibility for developing talent typically resides with the human resources function and senior executives are not held directly accountable for talent development. Finally, business leaders are typically not trained in coaching and developing others. To develop a talent pipeline, talent development efforts must be measured and rewarded and senior executives must be trained to coach and develop others."[8]

Another way that inspirational leaders champion supply chain excellence throughout the company is by establishing reward and incentive programs that encourage employees who contribute to supply chain process improvement. One insightful CEO gave both sales and supply chain people equal and shared responsibility for customer service and for inventory levels, knowing that both organizations played a major role in the decision process. Now when the sales managers complained about problems with customer availability, they knew they had to work with the supply chain group to come up with a creative solution, not simply make demands for more inventory.

One executive got it right when he noted, "The most inspirational leaders are those that win. Nothing beats winning to build morale and credibility in an organization." This supply chain professional cleverly planned the multiple projects in his company's transformation initiative in a way that guaranteed some quick and visible wins. He then built on that success and its cache of credibility to tackle the far more difficult cross-functional initiatives.

Technical Savvy

Technology has become a key enabler of supply chain excellence, and spending on supply management applications and services continues apace (covered in more detail in the next chapter). According to AMR Research, supply chain IT spending will continue to increase rapidly, up to 15 percent in any given year.[9] Indeed, in our work across hundreds of companies, including retailers, manufacturers, and service providers, we almost always see that the supply chain organization often consumes the majority of the IT spending, in support of warehouse management systems, transportation management systems, inventory management and production planning systems, and so on. Leaders must understand technology's contribution, both at broad and at quite detailed levels, to plan supply chain activities with precision, speed, and flexibility. That's the case whether it involves transportation routing software, tools for better managing supplier relationships, demand forecasting solutions, or sophisticated sales and operation planning packages.

The supply chain chief need not be credentialed in IT systems, but he or she must have a close working relationship with the CIO and ideally have no shortage of IT-savvy specialists on staff. He or she should have dealt with the challenges of technology selection, implementation, and application and be alert to the next-generation of technology tools, as well as wise to the implementation challenges inherent in the complexity of supply chain software solutions.

One supply chain professional told us about a mistake he made earlier in his career. He felt he did not have time to get into the technical details of a new system to allocate inventory to customers on a priority basis. (The company had never prioritized customers before and managed by reacting to complaints.) Instead, he delegated the specifics to staff members. Later he noted, "The devil really was in the details. I didn't think through how much conflict would arise when we tried to enforce customer priorities. My career hit the wall because I did not take the time to ask enough questions about this new technology, and especially how we were going to manage the political issues when people wanted to manipulate the priorities, which happened constantly. When major product shortages resulted for key customers, I was blindsided. All the fingers of blame pointed at me, and I had no defense. I will never make that mistake again."

One other sea change is under way—the migration of production, IT, and business processes to outsourced service providers. The trend is particularly relevant to supply chain professionals in the case of third-party logistics providers (3PLs) that manage warehousing and transportation operations for companies. In managing 3PLs, relationship management is becoming prized as a core skill. Although innate interpersonal skills will carry a supply chain professional a long way in collaborating with 3PLs, disciplined processes and systems for managing and guiding those relationships are essential.

Superior Business Skills

Supply chain leaders must be businesspeople first and supply chain specialists second. Their foremost focus must be on enhancing economic profit and shareholder value, not simply on cost cutting. Supply chains enhance economic profit by looking at everything from asset productivity to revenue generation. As one senior supply chain executive told us, "In manufacturing or sales, the cause/effect of cost or sales performance is often clearer and even intuitively understood. But in a cross-functional supply chain, you have to essentially model a series of complex interdependencies to understand which button to push."

Supply chain leaders must be able to speak the language of senior executives as easily as they can talk about fleet-truck efficiencies or demand forecasting. Terms such as EBITDA, ROIC, and economic profit should be part of their everyday parlance, and supply chain leaders should be as comfortable discussing cash flow with the treasurer's office as they are with talking about delivery schedules with suppliers. Supply chain issues are often the least understood by the board and the CEO, and must be explained in their language.

Analytical thinking is an essential component of the business skills mix, meaning that the supply chain leader must be driven far more by facts than by gut feel. He or she must be able to quickly find useful patterns in data, communicate them clearly, and act on the findings, in short, to be able to turn information into insight. Supply chain leaders who have worked as consultants often have a good grounding in such approaches.

One CEO shared his recent experience in interviewing several candidates for chief supply chain officer. One stood far above the others, mainly due to her ability to discuss overall business strategy with the CEO. She peppered him with queries about the customers, the marketing and brand strategies, and the nature of the board of directors. She wanted to understand in detail the CEO's own objectives, the ones that really drove his bonus. As the CEO said, "She had a real feel for the entire business and has made an invaluable member of my executive team."

Finding Executives with Necessary Skills

No particular industry has a monopoly on these five skills. But could supply chain expertise limited to just one specific industry be a deal breaker when hiring a supply chain executive? In our work with hundreds of firm, we are amazed at how supply chain expertise carries across very disparate industries. For example, in our projects ranging from lipstick to jet planes (Estée Lauder to Lockheed Martin), we found executives dealing with the same cross-functional, cross-company supply chain issues. Therefore, specific industry expertise should not be a prerequisite, as long as the executive has deep supply chain expertise. Plenty of latitude exists to bring in supply chain leaders from other industry sectors. For example, we recently saw a supply chain professional move very successfully from a hard-goods manufacturer to a retailer, and another successfully move from a retailer to a global manufacturer. Core supply chain expertise transcends specific industries.

Assembling a Talented Team

Demand for the most talented supply chain professionals will continue to rise, and hiring and retaining them will continue to tax the best organizations. Companies must "sell the opportunity" to candidates much more adroitly. What must CEOs and their organizations do to ensure that they have the supply chain experts who can drive true strategic success? First, they must create the right environment, then acquire the very best supply chain talent available, and finally, aggressively develop that talent.

Create the Right Environment

First, companies must shift from functional leadership roles to process-wide supply chain management. They must redefine the role of the supply chain functional leader to include responsibility to coordinate the end-to-end process. To do this effectively, supply chain leaders should report directly to the CEO and be closely involved with strategic direction, including inorganic growth through mergers and acquisitions. Supply chain management can deliver significant benefits in the form of outstanding product availability; reduced working-capital investment; and faster inventory turns, lower fixed costs and greater return on assets. But it can do this only if recognized as a complex, technology-driven discipline that must be approached holistically across functions, business processes, and corporate boundaries.

Second, companies must define the supply chain role and its link to business strategy. It is crucial to communicate within the organization and with critical business partners exactly what the supply chain process means, how far upstream it extends toward customers, and how far downstream it reaches through the tiers of suppliers. In general, firms must accept that the supply chain process extends end to end, from suppliers to customers, and across functional boundaries. The broad meaning of the supply chain then must be communicated widely and reinforced in every subsequent supply chain activity. The definitions become the foundation for everything from supply chain job descriptions to the language of collaboration used with third-party logistics providers.

Acquire the Best Talent

Next, companies must enter the contest for talent after carefully determining the right mix of functional proficiencies and the right combination of the five universal characteristics discussed earlier. Engaging in the battle for scarce talent involves viewing the world, other industries, and supply chain management training programs as the talent basket. Supply chain management is no longer limited by national borders or industry boundaries. Leading practitioners consider the world their talent basket, and they extend their searches accordingly to India, Australia, the Philippines, South Korea, Mexico, and beyond.

David Speer, chairman and CEO of Illinois Tool Works, a diversified manufacturer of advanced industrial technology, is clearly aware of the competition for global talent, "I think there is a huge challenge not only in trying to grow in a variety of international markets and settings but in attracting and retaining the kind of people you need to be effective in diverse cross-cultural organizations."[10]

Develop Internal Talent

Finally comes the need to develop talent for key supply chain process roles, which involves creating a professional development plan for every manager in the supply chain organization. Too many supply chain managers lack sufficient knowledge of how the rest of the company runs. CEOs should include their supply chain leaders in cross-functional businesswide decisions. In addition, they should encourage their supply chain staffs to take advantage of the wide range of educational opportunities available at universities and professional societies.

Leading firms create ways to develop the talent needed. Approaches may involve temporary and part-time positions, and underutilized practices such as circular migration, as is done at Procter & Gamble, with expatriates coming to the home office country, and those in the home office going abroad. Any global approach to talent will not succeed easily; it will require a major effort involving detailed planning of an array of leadership development initiatives.

Universities are stepping up not only with more appropriate education for the growing numbers of aspiring supply chain leaders, but with executive education programs that help shore up the business savvy of established supply chain specialists. When it comes to functional expertise, companies can do more to align and drive new phases of supply chain education at all levels. There is more room for universities to provide universal supply chain management skill sets.

CEOs know that managing the supply chain effectively is critical for corporate survival in a global marketplace. Now it is time for them to turn awareness into action by identifying and empowering the talent that can lead their organizations to increased profitability.

Conclusion

Acquiring, developing, and retaining the right talent is a critical element in building a world-class supply chain. Finding talent is a special challenge due to cross-company, cross-functional challenges. Therefore, the five key talent characteristics discussed are even more critical for supply chain executives. A talent plan is clearly an essential part of the strategy to drive supply chain excellence and economic profit. But, it is not enough. There are four more steps to include in your strategy to achieve supply chain excellence; we describe technology in the next chapter.

ACTION STEPS

1. Seek talented supply chain professionals who possess the five key characteristics of global orientation, systems thinking, inspiring and influential leadership, technical savvy, and superior business skills.

2. View the world as a talent basket and look for talent across industries.

3. Shift from a purely functional leadership role to enterprisewide supply chain process management.

4. Define the supply chain role broadly and link it to business strategy.

5. Define the right mix of functional proficiencies, competencies, and experience needed for each of the supply chain team members and compete aggressively for people with those skills.

6. Develop talent internally with a professional development plan for all employees.

4

Selecting the Appropriate Technology

THE NEXT STEP ALONG the pathway to building a strategy for supply chain excellence is to make sure your company chooses and successfully implements the right technology. Improperly understood or implemented, technology can cause severe damage rather than improvement, so you must be careful in selecting and applying it. In this chapter, you will learn what you must do to make technology part of your supply chain excellence strategy.

The Foundation of Competitive Advantage

Many firms have found that they can make major reductions in cost by leveraging their warehouse and transportation management systems, and using bar codes, advanced picking, and even

RFID technologies. Other firms have dramatically reduced inventory and improved customer service by using advanced planning and scheduling systems. Still others have saved millions by analyzing in-depth the facility network. Many companies have balanced the pain versus the gain of new technology and have achieved huge benefits. Properly applied, technology can be a major part of turning your supply chain into a generator of economic profit, enabling your company to cut cost and inventory as well as enhance customer service.

For example, in 2005, Coca-Cola Bottling Co. Consolidated drastically upgraded its demand-planning and collaboration capabilities with a new inventory management process supported by software from JDA Software Group. Coca-Cola Bottling reduced inventory levels by 50 percent, while improving fill rates by 15 percent, and won Sam's Club Supplier of the Year award in 2006. In addition, it simultaneously absorbed a staggering 300 percent increase in product offerings. This drove an economic profit surge by greatly reducing assets, while supporting growth in revenue due to the enhanced product availability.

Black & Decker implemented a demand- and master-planning technology and saw a major improvement in forecast accuracy. But, more importantly, that translated into a huge reduction in production cycle time—from two weeks to four hours. As a result, it improved order fill rates to major customers like Home Depot and Lowe's, while being able to hold less inventory than their competitors. Again, this stoked the economic profit engine as fill rates supported revenue growth, while inventory was reduced.

Pain versus Gain

A wide array of supply chain technology exists, and the benefits can be huge. Yet serious risks lurk nearby. For example, a supply chain professional from a retailer specializing in children's toys told of trying to implement a new fulfillment system that went far over schedule and budget. The Christmas spike exploded before the fulfillment system was complete, resulting in an inability to process orders. People throughout the company worked fifty days straight, including Sundays, to try to stay ahead, yet the firm was forced to send thousands of letters saying, "Sorry, your toy order will not arrive before Christmas."

In another alarming example, a candy maker spent over $100 million installing a new supply chain decision support system. The "go-live" for this project slipped from April to September. As the Halloween spike approached, the firm pushed the system into operation before it was ready and subsequently missed $150 million of sales. The stock dropped 45 percent. In yet another situation, a shoe manufacturer installed a complex new system to run its supply chain. Again, there were major delays. The company's CEO announced that there would be a $100 million sales shortfall due to the new software, causing the stock to fall 20 percent.

Is there a fundamental cause at the root of these problems? One theory holds that supply chain projects fail due to a lack of internal collaboration (which we discuss in detail in chapter 5). In some firms, the supply chain organization simply doesn't have a broad enough span of control to drive the improvements needed, with supply chain functions fragmented throughout the organization. In a home appliance manufacturer, for example, manufacturing, procurement, logistics, and planning all report to totally different functional vice presidents. On the other hand, in concerns like the parts and service division of Cummins Inc., the leader of the global supply chain organization has broad authority for manufacturing, procurement, logistics, and planning. Clearly, this facilitates project success, although it's only one variable in the mix.

Another hypothesis endorses the idea that failure results from overfocusing on the technology, not on the underlying process changes. Projects often fall short due to change management deficiencies, not technical or process problems. Some firms have a culture of driving so relentlessly to meet schedule and budget that they often skip the soft, but ironically more important change management tasks. "On time, on budget, but not used" does not equal success.

This chapter leaves the details of that technology to other sources and will instead focus on the keys to managing supply chain technology. (Chapter 7 covers the topic of change management with practical advice on how to implement supply chain projects.) With the relentless advances in technology, supply chain professions have no choice but to leverage new technology to avoid competitive disadvantage. The landscape of supply chain technology can be intimidating. As indicated in the examples, firms face the real danger of a failed application that can severely cripple them along with the careers of supply chain and other executives. Before we discuss how to avoid the pitfalls, a high-level review of the supply chain technology landscape is in order.

Supply Chain Technology: What's New?

It is useful to think of technology in four buckets: software, e-business technologies, visibility and productivity, and process advances (as outlined in chapter 2 and summarized in table 4-1).

By including process advances in the table, we do not mean to lump them together with conventional technology. In fact, we feel that processes should be addressed first and then enabled later with software and other technology.

Firms vary widely in applying such technologies. For example, in our experience, over half of all warehouses still run on paper-based, manual systems, but many others have adopted the most advanced warehouse management software and product location and tracking technologies. Generally, larger firms implement more sophisticated technologies, but not always. For example, a $1 billion automotive parts manufacturer still warehouses

TABLE 4-1

Summary of supply chain technology categories

Technology category	Description
Software	Includes IT systems for activities such as forecasting, transportation, warehousing, inventory management, collaboration, etc.
e-business technologies	Includes such technologies as automatic ship notices, EDI, Web portals, electronic invoicing, and payment tied to shipping, etc.
Visibility and productivity	Consists of technologies such as advanced bar codes, RFID, voice- and light-picking systems, event management, etc.
Process advances	Includes process advances applied to the entire end-to-end supply chain, such as lean manufacturing, six sigma, collaborative planning, forecasting, and replenishment, etc.

thousands of SKUs without even using bar codes. Yet technology is waiting to explode. AMR Research forecasts a major increase in spending on supply chain management applications.[1]

What is the next big thing that will shape supply chain technology? We believe it will be technology that clearly drives economic profit, both short term and long term, and it will be heavily influenced by the external environment. For example, if transportation costs in the long run increase much faster than overall inflation, companies will need to apply increasingly powerful technology that can answer such questions as these:

- What are the best locations for my warehouses?

- How should I place inventory in the network?

- How can I plan transportation to minimize cost and maximize service?

If future customers require more choice and customization, firms will need to handle and react to increasingly large volumes of data and customize supply chain service and product solutions for individual markets. As software capability continues to advance, availability of leading software solutions will become more convenient with concepts such as "software as a service" (SaaS). Optimization technology will also become more prevalent, allowing firms to maximize economic profit while simultaneously considering constraints such as customer product-availability requirements.

Kevin O'Marah, chief strategy officer of AMR Research, says, "The most important emerging technology is the enormously powerful data processing capability available today. Very complex problems can be solved in minutes, not hours or days. Huge simulation and optimization engines can be built practically today."[2] The assumptions of executives about what is possible can become obsolete almost overnight. Therefore, staying abreast of the rapidly changing technology environment is imperative.

Senior Executives and Supply Chain Technology

Senior executives play a critical role in ensuring that technology contributes rather than hampers a strategy for supply chain excellence. They must have a good knowledge of supply chain technologies and of plans to apply the new technologies. More importantly, the supply chain leader and staff must ask the right challenging questions about supply chain technologies. (Seven questions senior executives should ask are listed at the end of the chapter in table 4-2.) Senior executives have to become involved because a misapplication of technology can cause a supply chain disruption tearing at the basic fabric of the firm, as illustrated in the previous examples.

In an analysis of 827 supply chain disruptions, researchers found that stock price declined an average of 40 percent from peak to trough.[3] Technology can provide a distinct competitive advantage, but it can also severely damage a firm's supply chain. This happens when companies fail to apply the three rules we discuss next for successfully implementing supply chain technology. By asking a few simple questions (detailed below) at the beginning of a technology project, senior executives can reduce the risk of implementing supply chain technology.

Three Rules for Successful Implementation

The three important rules for successfully implementing new supply chain technology can apply to almost any new technology in any area. But the complexity of supply chain issues, with their huge impact on economic profit and share price, make these rules even more critical to follow.

Rule One: Use Leading-Edge (Beta) Technology Appropriately

Beta technology refers to new technology not yet fully debugged. The complexity of global supply chains often pushes supply chain executives to the limits of new technology. One supply chain executive from a retailer said he felt strongly that the only way to maintain an industry advantage was to strike while a technology was still very new, "How else can I get a competitive advantage?" An executive from another retailer, competing in many of the same product lines, related how his firm critically needed an inventory-allocation capability not available with existing software. He felt his only option was to partner with a software firm to develop this capability. He knew that such software simply did not exist and had no choice but to pursue the new technology if he was going to address a critical business objective and customer requirement.

To engage in a beta implementation, firms must have an appetite for projects with no definite end or set budget. Yet ironically, supply chain executives must often meet very demanding and disciplined business targets, with definite schedules and budgets, creating a challenging dilemma.

Fast-Follower Strategy

While the innovation approach clearly holds great potential value, a supply chain executive in a very cost-competitive industry told us passionately that he felt he lost very little by implementing quickly once a new technology stabilized. He strongly argued that it was far better to let the early adopter expend all the time and money to debug the new technology, and then dive in when it is cheaper and faster to implement.

The majority of senior executives do not easily tolerate projects with indefinite time lines and budgets, and many companies have a culture with a low tolerance for risk. Proposing beta projects in such an environment can damage careers as well as the firm itself. Those companies should avoid beta technology. And, of course, firms with severely limited financial resources should also adopt a fast-follower strategy.

A Beta Surprise

Regardless of the culture, a hidden danger exists. Sometimes an overhyped technology may not appear on the surface to be an immature beta version, when in fact it is. After buying based on an exaggerated sales pitch, one clearly frustrated and angry project manager said she thought she was getting stable production-planning technology. She found out too late as the project encountered bug after bug that the software marketing promises were overblown. She had to constantly explain to her very disappointed boss why the project was still not finished. To avoid this problem, project leaders should ask for references on at least one other company using the new technology and follow up on any references.

In another example, a frustrated supply chain manager told us about his boss, who fancied himself an innovator. Unfortunately, the boss consistently succeeded in confusing the organization. The manager said that his boss heard a colleague in another firm brag about implementing a "demand signal repository" (to store and manage point of sale data). Caught in the neat buzzwords, the boss wanted to make sure he maintained his image of being on the leading edge. He launched an initiative to implement the technology and less than sixty days later, he lost interest when the next new idea appeared. Subordinates in this organization, who said he repeatedly did things like this, termed the behavior "whack-a-mole management." He continually jumped from bandwagon to bandwagon, never letting what seemed like a good idea pass by without churning his organization. "Focus and complete" beats "launch and leave" every time. This holds especially true for complex global supply chains in which it is all too easy to stray from the strategy and chase the operational problem or the technology of the day.

Whether a firm has the tolerance for beta technology or not, it is unforgivable if the firm discovers it is on the leading, untested edge in the middle of the initiative, as did the project manager in the previous example. This unfortunately is all too common with supply chain projects. For example, during a supply chain audit, we heard from a supply chain executive about how a new inventory decision support system was going to solve a lot of problems. Six months later, at a supply chain forum meeting, we asked how the project was going. He sheepishly admitted that had he known he would be on the "bleeding edge," he would never have approved the project. He was two months past schedule and didn't want to think about the budget situation. Of course, he was getting huge pressure from his boss and was worried that things could get worse before they got better. In retrospect, he knew he should have asked the critical question, "Who else has implemented this technology, and have we spoken with them?"

In another case, the leader of a project team told us about glowing reports from a software sales representative on the capability of a new transportation planning application. However, four months into implementation, major problems with unstable software surfaced with a vengeance. The team finally did some research and found that claims of implementation in other firms were simply untrue. At best, some customers were currently involved in difficult implementations. They could not find a truly live, stable environment. The project team members learned the hard way that they needed to do more research at the beginning of the project. They found too late that they could not trust the claims of the software vendor.

Bleeding Edge to the Leading Edge

Some firms partner with a technology supplier to develop an application for addressing a unique need in the supply chain area, fully expecting the difficult journey ahead. They fundamentally believe that once ahead of competition, they can stay ahead. As they work with a supply chain software developer, the software product takes on the character of their unique processes. A supply chain executive told us how he partnered with a leading software firm to develop a warehouse management application that allowed his company's customers to be segmented into groups, enabling his firm to implement a different customer service strategy for each group. This gave the firm a distinct advantage by having a service plan tailored to each customer. The executive expected that the project would be a long-term effort and was not surprised when unforeseen events occurred, delaying the project for months. In this kind of an environment, the beta project thrived and eventually yielded a very powerful leading-edge application for his firm.

Recently, we asked a supply chain executive why she decided to implement new, untested software to assign inventory to customer orders. She told us that she didn't really like leading-edge projects, but sometimes they were the only way to accomplish a required business objective. When her firm's largest customer demanded priority service, she presented the problem to her technical staff. This customer represented over 20 percent market share for the firm. Yet the system used at the time to handle thousands of orders per day operated on a first-come, first-serve basis. After reviewing the capabilities available, her staff reported that the request was not doable with currently available technology from the software supplier and changing to a new supplier would be a huge undertaking. She then agreed to a development project, striking a partnership with the technology supplier. She agonized over the fact that this added a lot of complexity to the process, violating her usual principle of striving to keep processes as simple as possible. In the end, she felt that the customer requirement dominated. As she told us, "Sometimes meeting customer demands means you have no choice but to live on the edge."

Rocket Science

A barrier that confronts firms as they decide how close to the leading edge they dare tread is the availability of qualified people. As one supply chain executive observed, "This stuff really is rocket science!" AMR Research believes that close to 100 percent of companies do not have sufficient talent to smoothly implement leading-edge supply chain technology projects.[4] Supply chain talent in general is rare (as we discussed in chapter 3), but supply chain expertise *and* the ability to handle the new software technology are especially rare. The competition for this talent is intense for the limited resources available.

Lead or Follow?

In summary, companies with risk-avoidance cultures should avoid beta projects in the supply chain area and adopt a strategy to follow once the technology stabilizes. On the other hand, firms that can tolerate higher risk have the opportunity to develop a successful application and competitive advantage. But in both cases, the most unforgivable sin is to be in the middle of an implementation and suddenly and surprisingly learn that the technology is beta and has not been successfully implemented anywhere.

Rule Two: Realize That People Issues Are Tougher Than Technical Issues

People issues are always the toughest, but in the supply chain arena, cross-functional and cross-company issues add a much higher dimension of complexity. Often, completing the technical tasks is the easy part of an implementation. All the principles of disciplined project management must be in place, with excellent leadership. But the tougher issue involves getting people to use and embrace the new supply chain technology.

For example, a supply chain retail executive told us that his company recently implemented a $25 million software package to do inventory planning, with the new software to be used by the firm's buyers. The buyers reported to merchandising, but the supply chain people were asked to lead the implementation, since they had the overall accountability for inventory management. The software was truly state of the art and used optimization techniques involving some very sophisticated underlying mathematics.

A couple of weeks after the go-live date, the supply chain executive walked through the area where the buyers were working so he could get a feel for how they were using the new system. On every screen, he noticed an Excel spreadsheet. As soon as he returned to his office, he asked the project manager if the new system had Excel spreadsheets in it. The project manager admitted it did not. After further intense questioning, he found that the users still relied on Excel because they did not understand the new system. The buyers with little technical background had no chance of understanding the underlying mathematics and sophisticated logic, and had not even received proper training.

Therefore, when the new software produced illogical numbers, they had no clue what adjustments to make. To get orders out to the suppliers on time, their only choice was to rely on their old Excel spreadsheets and do the calculations offline. Then they would manually insert the answer into the new software. In effect, they had performed a complete bypass on a $25 million system, rendering it worthless.

A Plan for Changing People

How could the situation described in the example happen? Studies show that people challenges, not technical issues, pose the greatest danger to a new supply chain technology implementation. Senior supply chain executives must have a change management plan for all new projects and especially those involving new technology. The plan must lay out the process for gaining full organization buy-in and for in-depth training. Senior executives need to have confidence that the supply chain leaders will step away from their offices, wade into the operation, and relentlessly follow up to ensure the change management plan is executed successfully.

According to our data, people management represents the most important component of project success. That's why we've covered it in much more detail in chapter 7.

Software to Match the Needs of the Line Operation

The supply chain includes many line operations that may be vulnerable to corporate staff selecting a technology solution without line buy-in. For example, a warehouse manager had a close call with some new technology that could have caused a real problem. The corporate supply chain staff went along with the recommendation of the corporate IT organization and selected new order-picking technology for his warehouse. Although the technology was perhaps good for the large warehouses in the company, the warehouse manager felt that it was far more than his operation needed and would result in a cost increase, causing him to miss his cost targets. When he complained, the corporate departments told him to "change your processes to be consistent with the new technology, because we want everyone to be on the same system."

At this point, the line manager faced two choices. He could try to live with it, or he could make it an issue, with both approaches involving some risk to his operation and to him personally. He summoned the courage to choose the latter course, put together a compelling story, and presented it to his director. Fortunately, the director had a long history of front-line experience and understood immediately. The project was halted soon thereafter. The corporate staff groups and their leaders who had sponsored the new technology lost a lot of career credibility. They could have avoided this mess if they had taken the time to listen to the concerns of the line managers.

Technology projects should provide new capability to help supply chain line operations cut cost, reduce working capital, or improve product availability, thus enhancing economic profit. The process owners of critical line applications in the supply chain such as transportation, warehousing, inventory management, order management, and demand forecasting systems are the ones who will use the technology after it is implemented. Therefore, they must lead the implementation project.

User Unfriendliness

Often, supply chain processes and systems become so complex that no single person understands everything. Sometimes technical people become irrelevant due to their own arrogance. For example, a sales manager in a farm supplies business said that with a recent major systems implementation, he lost sight of inventory levels. He angrily said, "We were selling blind. I literally have no idea what is in stock." When we asked the supply chain people what happened, they said there was actually a straightforward approach to getting this information out of the new system: "We showed that guy how to do it!" The sales manager confirmed that the supply chain folks demonstrated the system to him once, but he found it to be much too complex when he tried it himself and gave up. Needless to say, the supply chain organization needs to involve other functions like sales early in any technology effort.

During a supply chain audit, production planners in an apparel company described a production planning system that had five different tools, depending on the situation, which created an incredibly complex process for them that no one fully understood. They used one special tool for high-volume "super A" products; second, they had to apply an ABC volume segmentation of the product; next they were required to run an inventory tool to calculate desired safety stock inventory; and the fourth step involved reviewing real customer orders to make sure they reacted to any unmet needs. If this weren't enough, a pull approach was being piloted for some product lines. For every product type, they were required to use a different scheduling technique and, in some cases, more than one.

Complex technology should not look complex to the users. The people struggling with the demands of daily line problems do not have time to troubleshoot technology. A key question should be, "Will the new technology make line jobs harder or easier?" Murphy's law guarantees that things will go wrong with new technology, especially in the complex, interdependent supply chain world. When this happens, people need to fall back on their training and their support system. Did senior managers ensure that sufficient training was done and done at the right time? Did they ensure the availability of adequate support available from the vendor when problems inevitably arise?

The Toyota plant in Georgetown, Kentucky, approaches new technology differently. For example, several years ago, people pedaled three-wheel bikes around the plant, manually picking up the cards requesting more material (known as *kanban* cards) and taking them to materials control to request a resupply of needed component material. When asked why they just didn't send an electronic signal to the materials area requesting the material, they explained that they wanted to keep the flows visible and understandable to the workforce. That way, the employees generated more and better ideas for improvement. They believed that sometimes technology creates such a complex operation that people no longer understand the way the place works and therefore cannot offer ideas for improvement. Now Toyota has reconciled needs like this with extensive training and is more comfortable using electronic signals. Toyota continually seeks ways to balance the need for user simplicity with the promise of a new technology.

Rule Three: Ensure That the Technology Project Has a Business Case

One key theme of this book is that supply chain excellence generates the most important commodity in the boardroom: economic profit. Therefore, every supply chain technology project should be put in terms of economic profit.

Benefits Not Quantified Equal Worthless Benefits

Senior executives should understand that line supply chain people often struggle with quantifying the benefits of their new technology proposals and do themselves a great disservice in the process. Senior executives should make clear that if a project team fails to quantify a benefit, that benefit is treated effectively as zero. For example, one CEO described a project designed to save $11 million in cost and also improve product availability. He continued to be chagrined throughout multiple reviews that only the $11 million received any attention. Ironically, he knew that the improvement of availability would be the far greater benefit, but it was effectively ignored because no dollar value was attached. He strongly urged the supply chain group to get creative and quantify all benefits. Then once quantified, they further had the responsibility to continually remind the organization of the benefit at stake as the project progressed.

A supply chain executive in a manufacturing company understood this very well. She mentored her team in developing a business case for a major supply chain decision support system. She was determined to show the project's impact on economic profit. The business case for the initiative called for a $110 million inventory reduction, a $12 million freight-cost reduction, and a four-point improvement in the availability percentage from 92 percent to 96 percent. Her team worked hard to get sales to agree that the availability percentage improvement would translate into a one-point improvement in market share, yielding another $25 million in bottom-line profits. The supply chain executive then became almost legendary in her company for beginning every meeting during the next thirteen months reminding everyone of the commitment to achieving these savings. She gave exactly the same speech word for word at the beginning of every meeting. Not only was it impossible for people to forget the promised benefits, but after several months, they said they could quote them in their sleep. She even translated the benefits into economic profit and led the CEO to understand the positive impact on share price that the initiative could drive.

The executive realized that after project sign-off, the organization focuses on the tasks required to get the project done. As the intensity of task completion increases, she knew the team members could easily forget why they were doing the project. She made sure that did not happen.

Cost and Benefit Compared to What?

Few supply chain managers have an aptitude for developing a solid business case. For example, a supply chain manager at a retail chain said that he seemed to read an article on RFID almost every day. He felt that his company would fall behind if it did not quickly embrace this new technology. He did a quick analysis of the implementation cost and put together a proposal for a pilot project that involved a reasonably modest effort. He felt his boss would jump at the chance to stay abreast of market leaders.

When he presented the proposal to his boss, she asked the correct question, "What is the business case for RFID?" He realized that he had a good handle on the cost, but had not bothered to quantify the benefit. Feeling humbled by this oversight, the project manger hurried to identify and quantify benefits. He felt that RFID would generate benefits such as better tracking and inventory control, reducing inventory investment, and improving order fill rates. He put some estimates together to fully quantify the cost versus the benefit. Feeling confident, he hurried back to his boss, proudly showing her the complete business case.

His boss then asked another excellent question, "What is the business case versus the next-best option?" Initially confused, he quickly realized that most of the new functionality could actually be delivered by advanced bar-code technology. Looking at the incremental cost and the incremental benefit of RFID versus the alternative of a bar-code system caused the business case to virtually disappear.

The supply chain executive knew the right questions to ask about a new technology. In this situation, she elected to proceed with RFID for strategic reasons, but at least she knew the facts. Unfortunately, in all too many cases, a glamorous initiative gains momentum on hype, not substance, and once set in motion seems to have a life of its own.

In another example, a project team proposed installing a warehouse system to guide the work of picking products for orders. The team members wanted a "voice picking" system in which the workers would wear headsets and a computer-generated voice would guide them in picking the items for an order. The supply chain senior executive reviewed the business case and was initially impressed with the productivity improvement and the return on investment promised by the team. However, he had just visited a Dell operation where he saw an order-picking system that seemed simpler and less costly. In that system, workers were guided to areas by small lights indicating which product they should pick for an order (i.e., a pick-to-light system). He asked the team for the cost benefit of voice picking versus a pick-to-light approach. The voice-picking approach still won the day because it excelled in the accuracy so extremely important in this application. But the team was now grounded in an approach that they knew was right for the next decade.

Eliminate Before You Automate

Another example involves a business case based on a totally incorrect premise. A supply chain director for a farm machinery maker told us that the materials group implemented the latest automated storage and retrieval system (ASRS) technology to warehouse parts in its factories. This was a high-rise warehouse, with a robot to put away and pick material. Later the group found that it could have totally avoided the expense of the system. They devised a way to take material *directly* from the receiving docks to the point of use in the factory, totally avoiding the high-rise automated warehouse.

For several years, on plant tours, the group would show guests the automated storage and retrieval system. But the unique thing was that it was *empty*. They referred to it as "the epitome of a monument to waste," explaining that it was far better to eliminate the handling of inventory rather than automate it. "Eliminate before you automate" became a common mantra in this firm. Automated storage and retrieval systems definitely have their place. But a key question to ask is whether the fundamental need for the new technology can be eliminated by redesigning the process.

Seven Questions About New Technology

As these examples show, many dangers await the unsuspecting supply chain leader asked to approve a new supply chain technology implementation. But if supply chain professionals and others in management up to the CEO ask seven key questions at the beginning of any supply chain technology project, many of the pitfalls of failed implementation can be mitigated if not avoided entirely. The seven key questions to ask, especially for supply chain projects, and the actions to take are shown in table 4-2.

TABLE 4-2

Questions supply chain leaders and senior executives should ask before acquiring or implementing supply chain technology

Question	Action
1. Who else has implemented this supply chain technology, and have you spoken with them?	If this has not been done, stop the project until it is.
2. Are you implementing a cross-functional change management communication plan and is it tailored to the individuals and functions critical to this effort?	This has to be done. Ask to see the written plan with dates, assigned responsibilities, and a time line.
3. Will this make line jobs in the supply chain easier or more complex?	If easier, great. The answer is more likely to be "more complex." If more complex, make sure there is a clear training program and a clear return on the investment supported by those who are doing the real work.
4. Do you have a plan for sustaining the cross-functional change once it is made?	If not, write it up, make assignments, and hold people accountable for date-driven tasks.
5. What is the complete business case to generate economic profit for this project?	Make sure the benefit is quantified and clearly communicated.
6. What is the business case vs. the next-best option to generate economic profit?	A tough but necessary question. If asking this makes your ROI disappear, you have a problem. Stop the project and evaluate further.
7. Can we eliminate the need for the technology by eliminating non-value-added supply chain operations?	Eliminate before you automate.

Conclusion

Supply chain technology is a critical, enabling step toward building a strategy for supply chain excellence. There are major tools to apply if a firm is to compete successfully in the supply chain arena. As we discussed, there are myriad possible pitfalls that can be avoided by following our advice. With the systems and process advances of the past decade, we see many firms making major advances in driving down operating cost, cutting working capital, improving product availability, and enhancing revenue—all key components of economic profit. With technology and talent, we have two steps of our supply chain strategy in place. But there are three more to consider. Next, we turn to the area of collaboration, both internal and external collaboration, covered in the next two chapters.

ACTION STEPS

1. Stay abreast of supply chain technical capability as it rapidly changes and advances.

2. Avoid the three deadly sins of implementing new supply chain technology: incorrectly applying beta technology, underestimating people issues, and having a weak business case to drive economic profit.

3. Ask seven key questions about any new technology at the beginning of any supply chain technology project.

5

Collaborating Internally

AFTER TALENT AND TECHNOLOGY, the third step toward the strategy to drive supply chain excellence is internal collaboration. Successful collaboration occurs when sales, marketing, and operations find a way to align and focus on serving the customer in a way that maximizes economic profit. This chapter presents examples of success as well as dysfunctional behavior. Each function in the firm plays a critical role in a successful supply chain, and this chapter will help you see how they can work together to achieve supply chain excellence. In addition, at the end of the chapter, there is an assessment test for you to complete so you can honestly evaluate your company's process for aligning the demand and supply sides—the sales and operations planning (S&OP) process.

The Curse of Functional Silos

Functional silos exist in every firm. They are not necessarily bad, because they serve as a foundation to build deep process expertise and as a vehicle for firm accountability. The problem occurs when they become barriers to supply chain excellence. In building a strategy for excellence, the important point is to understand how impermeable the functional silos can be to a smoothly operating supply chain. At the University of Tennessee, we offer a supply chain audit service that involves extensive analysis of company data, followed by many interviews inside the firm and interviews with customers and suppliers. Then the audit compares the findings to a database of best practices consisting of over 500 companies. The eight most recent supply chain audits in our database include:

- A major automotive manufacturer

- A major defense contractor

- A leading cosmetics firm

- An automotive parts manufacturer

- A pet supplies maker

- An apparel maker

- A large tire producer

- An industrial pump supplier

Company size in the sample ranges from $100 million in annual sales to over $30 billion. Although the firms audited are tremendously diverse and profitable, they all suffer from functional silo problems ranging from moderate to severe. As one frustrated executive said, "How can you manage horizontally when you are organized vertically?" The supply chain process is the ultimate horizontal process, with links stretching from suppliers across the firm to customers. Even within the firm, the interfaces require a daunting degree of coordination from product design to marketing, procurement, manufacturing, logistics, and sales, enabled by finance and IT.

The CEO at the Eye of the Storm

Only the CEO can make sure all functions in the company are on the same page. The supply chain leader must help the CEO and the executive team understand that if they want to move toward a world-class supply chain capability, all areas of the company need to be rowing in the same direction with the same cadence. This takes an intense dedicated effort to bridge the inevitable gulf between the operations and the revenue-generation sides of the company. The CEO must take on the burden of cross-functional alignment to avoid the curse of functional silos and the crippling impact on the supply chain.

In a consumer products firm we audited, the CEO made a valiant attempt to overcome entrenched functional silos by eliminating all offices. He set up his own work area as a desk in the middle of a large, open bay. He could stand up and see his vice presidents scattered around the room. But still the problem persisted. As long as misaligned objectives drove his vice presidents' compensation, the location of their desks really didn't matter.

At a hard-goods company, the senior executive team tried to address the functional silo problem by creating a cross-functional business team, called the operations management team (ops team). The team consisted of director-level members from each function. They met weekly to make the tactical supply-and-demand management decisions required to guide the firm throughout the year. Each member of the team held a big stake in its successful performance. Forty percent of their individual rating on an overall evaluation depended on the performance of the ops team in delivering cost reduction, inventory reduction, and product availability improvement. In our work with many firms, we rarely see this much motivation to align across functions. In spite of that, the underlying disease persisted. As one team member observed, "When the going got tough, the tough got functional." In other words, any conflict inevitably drove the players back to their functional sanctuaries.

This chapter is a road map for attacking the problem of disconnects that can cripple a firm's supply chain and is a key component of a strategy that delivers supply chain excellence. In our database of best practices, we have identified a number of approaches that are working. In this journey, we find that leading companies start at the beginning, with the initial design of their products.

Begin with Product Design

A world-class supply chain begins with the design of the product, and a world-class design starts with the customer. A well-known axiom in product design holds that once design engineering completes the product design, at least 80 percent of the product quality and cost are set. The suppliers and factory only affect, at most, the remaining 20 percent. It does little good to pressure manufacturing to improve cost or quality once it loses most of its freedom. In our experience, most manufacturing companies acknowledge this problem, and therefore most involve manufacturing in the product design process to address it. However, very few have taken the next step. Few companies seem to understand that the same principle also applies to supply chain's involvement in the design process.

Design for Flexible Turnaround and Changeover

Once the product design is set, not only manufacturing but the entire supply chain loses most of its flexibility. Product design dimensions and weight clearly have an impact on transportation and warehousing costs. Design also affects product availability. Just as engineers need to design for cost and quality, they also need to design for fast response to customer demand. If the design supports flexible turnaround and changeovers in both the factory and its suppliers, the company can respond much faster to unexpected changes in demand, and the supply chain can provide better availability. Unfortunately, few engineering organizations have that objective, perhaps because the concept is so nebulous on the surface. How can a product be designed for "fast response to customer demand"? One design concept that truly represents a breakthrough in product availability and inventory management is that of postponement, often supported by an easily assembled modular design. With a product design that supports postponement, firms delay the unique differentiation of an SKU until just before it is shipped.

Postponement means that the design of the product allows the final, unique identification of an SKU to be delayed and then customized once the demand is known. Dell is the classic example. Before Dell started selling to retailers, it built computers for most consumers after the order was placed. The order generated a bar code specifying the unique characteristics of the computer. The bar code triggered a picking system in which lights indicated the bins where parts needed to be picked (pick-to-light system) to allow the proper components to be selected and placed in a bin. Then a team assembled the specific computer in a small manufacturing cell.

Delaying SKU differentiation until late in the manufacturing process improves manufacturing flexibility tremendously. One manufacturing manager in a refrigerator factory lamented, "We differentiate SKUs from the first hit on the raw steel in the press room." Generic designs that can be differentiated late are the key to more flexible manufacturing and better ability to respond to consumers. The idea is to keep the different product variations as uniform as possible for as long as possible. Hewlett-Packard waits until it is time to ship printers in Europe before it customizes the language and the electrical plug connection. Engineers have always known that they need to design for cost and quality, but to support a world-class supply chain, they also need to design for fast response to demand.

Include Supply Chain in New Product Planning

Most firms have a stage-gate process to guide the introduction of new products. The stage-gate process consists of a series of gates, with each one consisting of a number of required deliverables before the project can proceed to the next stage. One durable goods company calls its stage-gate process C2C (consumer to consumer) to capture the idea that new products both start with the consumer and end with the consumer. Cummins Inc. calls its stage-gate process VPI (value package introduction). Honeywell uses the term VPD (velocity product development). Cooper Tire & Rubber Company's process is NPD (new product development). All firms have their own jargon, but the concept is the same.

Marketing and engineering dominated the early stage-gate processes. The first versions of the process completely overlooked supply chain issues. Unfortunately, the majority of firms in our database have made disappointingly little progress beyond that. However, a small but growing number now include supply chain considerations as required deliverables of the various gates. What supply chain issues should be considered in the new product introduction process? At a minimum, five questions that are critical to an efficient and effective supply chain must be addressed:

1. How can we design the product for ease of manufacturing?

2. How can we design the product to reduce warehousing and transportation costs?

3. Have we done everything we can to reduce component and finished-product complexity?

4. Can we design for postponement (i.e., delaying the commitment to a specific SKU until as late as possible in the supply chain)?

5. Do we have a plan to phase out old products and phase in the new in order to maintain excellent customer service and minimize obsolete inventory?

Crippling Cross-Functional Problems

Once new products are designed and introduced, four chronic cross-functional problems that can cripple a supply chain often emerge. They are (1) too much obsolete inventory, (2) excessive product complexity, (3) poor forecasts, and (4) ineffective demand management. Misaligned functional silos often hinder the ability of firms to deal with these problems.

Too Much Slow-Moving, Obsolete Inventory

Most companies struggle with the problem of disposing of obsolete products in a timely manner. The sales function is often measured on both revenue and margin generated and naturally resists wasting price reductions on slow-moving, obsolete merchandise. Unfortunately, obsolete products never become more valuable. They sit there month after month consuming cash and incurring inventory holding costs until the firm finally scraps them or sells them at a steep discount, sometimes literally years after, in a classic example of "pay me now . . . or pay me later."

When the senior executives at a major consumer durables manufacturer reviewed their inventory records with us during an audit, we found millions of dollars of products over three years old still sitting in their warehouses. Even worse, this inventory clogged up the warehouse operations of the company and consumed working capital dollars that could have been invested in the current models customers wanted. In this company, the sales function had no incentive to reduce obsolete inventory. This contrasts with a rare retailer whose CEO told us that he decided to put inventory carrying costs on the financial statements of the sales function. To manage margins, the sales organization now has to worry about the level of inventory and, especially, slow-moving, obsolete inventory.

Many firms behave like an apparel manufacturer we know of where only the planning function was held accountable for inventory levels and customer availability, even though it controlled neither the physical input to nor the output from inventory stocks. The firm saw lead times triple as product was outsourced to Asia. SKUs increased dramatically, and sales provided zero input to the ongoing forecasts. In spite of that, the planning function was in the extremely lonely position of being the only function on the line that had products available to fill customer orders. One day, the director of planning found himself in a meeting with the CEO and all functional heads. The CEO asked who was accountable for ensuring that there was adequate supply of products for the customer. Only the production planning director held up his hand. The CEO took the opportunity to educate his staff on their shared responsibility in terms they couldn't misunderstand. But he knew he had to go further. The next quarter, he required everyone around the table to include customer-order fill rates in their individual performance metrics.

Some firms engage in creative approaches to rid themselves of obsolete inventory. We have observed a wide array of programs. Some find ways to donate the products and take a major tax reduction. Even large firms sometimes use eBay to dispose of obsolete products. Whatever the approach, the best practice is an automated process, which rids the firm *each month* of products that don't sell. This avoids the periodic panic that hits many companies when they realize how much junk is clogging their supply chains.

Too Many SKUs

Few factors cripple the supply chain more than excessive product complexity. It is almost impossible to find a firm without an SKU problem. Virtually all admit that they carry too many SKUs and further concede that they lack a good process to eliminate under-performing products. As one executive noted, "Controlling SKUs is like eating liver. At some point, you have to stop moving it around on your plate and just dive in." The problem exists at the beginning *and* at the end of life. Once new products are introduced and excessive complexity is unleashed, it takes on a life of its own. Like a snowball gathering mass as it barrels downhill, the problem grows rapidly worse.

Why does product complexity gather momentum and get progressively worse in many firms? Amazingly, most companies do not have an end-of-life process for old SKUs. One executive made the comment we have heard echoed over and over, "We have no problem introducing new products, but we totally lack any hint of a process for killing them off." Fortunately, this problem can be solved with some cross-functional discipline. A few world-class companies have an end-of-life process, constantly flushing unproductive SKUs from the system. Some firms have implemented hard and fast rules such as, "If we add an SKU, we have to eliminate an SKU." Others force marketing to seek approval from the CEO and executive committee for an expansion of the model lines, requiring them to present a rigorous justification before SKUs are added. These processes, although rare, are quite effective.

A company in the health-care industry faced a severe problem of SKUs growing rapidly with no end in sight. Market forces and competition drove some of this increase. But executives in all functions admitted to us in interviews that a significant portion was unnecessary, fostered by undisciplined processes at both the beginning and end of product life. They eventually came to realize that rapidly growing SKUs would have a devastating impact on the supply chain. When an unbelievable twenty thousand more SKUs materialized in just three months, they told us that they reached a complexity tipping point as rapidly expanding product variety literally overwhelmed the operational capabilities of the firm, causing cost and inventory to rise and product availability to deteriorate rapidly. In the past, their supply chain had managed, with heroic effort, to change fast enough to accommodate SKU growth, although at the price of very high inventory levels. However, the warning signs were there. Manufacturing, logistics, and even the finance people inside the company expressed serious concern, predicting that this future environment could make the existing manufacturing process and indeed the entire supply chain obsolete. We heard the following comments from senior executives inside the firm.

- "SKU growth is the scariest part of my job. We are not prepared for it. Our only hope is that customers will push back due to their space constraints. We need an end-of-life process."

- "SKUs are a huge concern. We are choking on SKUs. It is a big disappointment that we have brought no discipline to this. We are pathetic at killing old products."

- "Even our customers are very concerned about SKU growth. They say SKU proliferation is killing them."

As with all problems, facing the demon is half the battle. The supply chain leader was able to convince management all the way up to the CEO that SKU growth was the root of the crisis in inventory and product availability. They launched processes at both the beginning and end of SKU life. Given the CEO's commitment, cross-functional misalignment became less of a barrier, especially when the vice president of marketing took over the leadership of managing SKUs. Logic demands that the function making the decision to add or delete SKUs should lead any SKU-reduction effort. Marketing, not supply chain, is generally that function. But supply chain people can help marketing in collaboratively supporting the effort, providing realistic facts and honest analysis. The CEO in this example now includes SKU reviews in his monthly staff meetings. The number of SKUs has leveled off and declined slightly, and all staff members understand the need for a disciplined SKU-management process.

The CEO, once convinced, supported the effort, and that made all the difference. Senior management support is critical for dealing with such cross-functional problems. This story plays out in company after company. For example, when a major tire company eliminated 25 percent of its SKUs, the CEO said, in our supply chain forum, that its major customers told him that they felt no impact. CEO support is clearly required to resolve cross-functional problems like SKU management.

Some firms have built-in advantages that they should leverage when managing SKUs. For example, automotive companies can manage SKU elimination through routine model-year changeovers. Pharmaceuticals and cosmetics firms are able to manage shelf life with pull dates on their products. Such opportunities should not be squandered.

Forecasting Problems

Forecasting problems can be mitigated in many ways, such as by reducing cycle time, by holding inventory back in the chain, or, of course, by improving forecast accuracy. In many companies, absolutely no process exists to integrate sales input into the forecasting process. Perhaps even worse, the inputs are "gamed."

Sometimes gaming leads to unrealistically high forecasts in order to push operations to make more products. Sometimes the guidance follows the low road, perhaps to sandbag the goals. Either way, the lack of a good demand signal creates havoc in the supply chain.

At a consumer packaged-goods manufacturer, no forecast input came from sales or merchandising, forcing production planning to rely almost solely on a statistical forecast. The director of production planning said he had made repeated attempts, and finally got some guidance, grudgingly provided by the product-line sales directors. Unfortunately, the input led to forecasts even more inaccurate than before. As product availability continued to deteriorate, the CEO realized something had to be done. After a number of discussions with the director of supply chain, he realized that he had to put teeth in the process and required that a forecast accuracy measure be included in the performance metrics of the sales organization. Although achieving revenue targets was still the primary goal of sales, this concentration on the forecast turned around the downward trend and resulted in a marginal improvement in the accuracy of the forecast. More importantly, it forced sales to get serious about a demand plan that aligned with the forecast.

World-class firms measure forecast accuracy by calculating the average percentage error regardless of whether the error is high or low (mean absolute percent error or MAPE). They also measure forecast bias to indicate whether the forecast is consistently high or low. They hold sales, marketing, and planning accountable for forecast accuracy.

One supply chain chief in a technology company surprised us when she resisted our recommendation to measure forecast accuracy. Her view was that forecast accuracy is affected by many factors beyond anyone's control. She thought it simply not fair to hold people accountable for something so clearly outside their control. Yet, in over forty forecasting audits we have done, the data shows that companies that rigorously measure the accuracy of the forecast and hold a range of people accountable for it have much better forecast accuracy and better supply chain performance.

A supply chain director for a hard-goods manufacturer told us that he abandoned the idea of getting specific numerical input from sales. The sales representatives simply did not appreciate the importance of time spent in the forecasting process when they were overwhelmed with other responsibilities. The reps believed that their job was to sell and that manufacturing should just "make what we sell." The director next tried to obtain sales input via an "unusual event form." The form served as a vehicle to gather input for the forecasting team any time a sales representative became aware of something that might affect the sales forecast (e.g., a retail promotion). However, some salespeople submitted the form for insignificant items or rumors, while others did not send it in at all, causing this process to slowly fade into oblivion.

The director told us that he could not get any traction for the real solution of assigning accountability to the salesforce for the accuracy of its forecasts. Finally, he found the right approach for the culture. He was successful in organizing a quarterly meeting at which sales directors provided directional input on the state of the marketplace. Rather than provide specific forecast quantities, they passed along vitally important information obtained from their work with the retailers regarding the health of the business as well as competitors' status. They discussed their logic for upcoming promotion programs. The meeting helped all parties better understand the general trends in the marketplace and with competition, as well as future promotion.

Demand Mismanagement

Providing input to a forecast is one thing; managing demand is quite another. Unfortunately, in most firms, the sales organization makes little effort to shift customer demand to comparable

SKUs when products are unavailable. A supply chain executive in a durable goods firm related a particularly egregious event. Overnight, sales developed an aggressive promotion plan to counter a recent fall in market share, given the serious discussion the sales vice president had with the CEO regarding that market share loss. The sales vice president announced the promotion with great fanfare and scheduled it to start in a couple of weeks and run during the month of July. Unfortunately, the factory had scheduled a two-week shutdown for the first half of July.

In most companies, few promotional campaigns are initiated by the salesforce in order to shape demand and better match current supply constraints. Of course, the glaring exception is Dell. As Dell executives say, "We sell what we make—price is the only variable." Pricing varies hour to hour on the Dell Web site to align supply with demand in real time. Of course, as Dell sells more and more through retailers, it is struggling to maintain the purity of this concept.

Another executive said that his firm had a "sell what's available today" plan for moving inventory. He pointed out, "Anyone can take orders without regard for product availability. But it takes some talent and discipline to focus on selling what's available today." When demand is aligned with real capacity constraints, the company optimizes economic profit by achieving the maximum level of product availability with the minimum level of cost and inventory. Matching supply with demand is perhaps the greatest of all cross-functional opportunities.

Matching Supply with Demand

Many cross-functional problems prevent supply chain excellence, but the greatest of all is the inability to match supply with demand. Some call it sales, inventory, and operations planning (SIOP) or demand-supply integration (DSI). Sales and operations planning (S&OP) is the most common term that firms use to describe a wide range of activities employed to match supply with demand. Many argue that the holy grail of cross-functional alignment is the *ability to match supply with demand*. Most but not all of the firms we work with seem to be trying to implement or improve the internal process to align supply with demand.

Whatever the name, the concept of matching supply with demand requires that all key functions in the firm reach consensus, a daunting task indeed. One executive told us in obvious frustration, "This is the process where sales and operations get along . . . right? . . . Yeah, right." An operations executive said, "Can't they see that running promotions when we don't have capacity is basically advertising for competition?" Firms travel a hard road in integrating supply with demand, but the internal collaboration journey is well worth the effort.

Why Is Matching Supply with Demand So Difficult?

This activity carries such a high degree of difficulty due to its cross-functional nature as it attempts to align sales, marketing, operations, logistics, procurement, and finance in a plan that balances supply with demand. A supply chain executive in a building supplies company once told us, "We used to invite sales to the S&OP meetings, but stopped because it just slowed down the process." Clearly such behavior misses the point. It's hard to do S&OP without the *S*.

During another recent supply chain audit, we interviewed a supply chain director in a consumer packaged-goods firm who said its S&OP process was not working. When asked what caused the problem, he ticked off several reasons, with some emotion. He believed it began with the fact that objectives and metrics were not aligned and in fact drove behavior in opposite directions. Each function followed its own agenda. The alignment meetings then became long agonizing affairs, and eventually key players stopped attending because nothing was really decided anyway. Furthermore, the meetings failed to have a clear agenda and instead dissolved into expediting meetings dealing with the crisis of the day, rather than the plan for the next month.

When we asked the supply chain executive what he would like to change if he had the power to change it, he listed five essential items:

1. Common metrics—"The sales and marketing people need to worry about cost and inventory, just as we operations people need to be concerned about revenue generation."

2. Disciplined meetings with tight agendas focused on strategic issues—"These sessions are not the place for managing a problem that occurred an hour ago. Further-more, the meetings should begin and end on time, and be only an hour long."

3. Credible, understandable data.

4. Mandatory participation of key players.

5. Support from the top, and that means the CEO.

We think he nailed it. Our experience with hundreds of firms reinforces that these five conditions are necessary, and when in place, they can result in many benefits, some of which are low cost and quick to implement. For example, a consumer packaged-goods firm saw an improvement in its forecast accuracy by almost 50 percent by implementing a very simple process change that had zero cost and was proposed in an S&OP meeting. Sales simply started communicating its promotion plans to the people doing the forecasting. Amazingly, this simple change would have never occurred were it not for a discussion in an S&OP meeting.

The CEO of one consumer durables company understood the power of S&OP and said that he asked the following questions of his S&OP group:

1. Who attends S&OP meetings? Do they know their responsibilities, and do they consider attendance mandatory?

2. Do at least director-level personnel from sales, marketing, production, logistics, and finance attend the meetings, or have they delegated it lower in the organization?

3. Are sales, marketing, production, logistics, and finance able to agree on supply and demand plans?

4. Is our S&OP process about balancing supply and demand, and on reaching a consensus, not finger-pointing?

5. Do we use the latest technology in forecasting systems to support the process?

6. Have we aligned the performance metrics of the S&OP process to the individual functional metrics of all of the participants?

7. Do you rotate senior leadership of the S&OP process periodically so all parts of the organization gain a perspective on how their individual input to the S&OP process contributes to the success of the company as a whole?

With the CEO asking questions like these, the organization became deeply committed to the S&OP process.

Scott Roy, collaboration planning manager at Blue Bunny, the frozen dessert maker, told us the following story about implementing S&OP:

In our company, demand planning is housed in the marketing department and supply planning is in logistics, but we have worked over the last eighteen months in building an environment of integration and cooperation. I don't think that we could be where we are today without a strong S&OP process led by a key member of senior management. We had S&OP for six years before this and were just going through the motions and not making any true integration advancements. Eighteen months ago we got a new sheriff in town and things began to change. He had the vision of what S&OP was all about. We then took steps of truly identifying our business execution strategy, driven by service-level expectations, operations policies. We also took aggressive steps in developing customer-service-driven inventory strategies. We moved from a one size fits all inventory–safety stock strategy to item-level settings based on the unique nature of the items and the markets that they go into. The settings are reviewed every two months.

We address tactical supply and demand issues each Monday in a cross-functional inventory planning and supply meeting. We also review key performance metrics each week as well as changes in the plans from supply or demand are reviewed and acted upon.

To make this all work, there needs to be constant communication and integration between supply and demand supported by senior management tied back into a functioning S&OP Process. For years, S&OP was purely communication based. It was not until it became action oriented and accountability driven did we get over the hump.

We haven't perfected this thing, but we have created a performance-tracing and an improvement-driven environment. S&OP is no longer the place you go to make the other guy look bad, but the place you go to make the company succeed.[1]

Best Practices for Demand and Supply Integration

Almost all firms we work with are implementing S&OP, or reimplementing S&OP after an earlier, less than successful effort. Consequently, we have built a rich database consisting of best and worst practices as firms continue to try to align functions around a common supply and demand plan.

Mark Moon, a professor at the University of Tennessee and a consultant for many firms that are striving to integrate supply with demand, has created a process of best practices for S&OP (see figure 5-1).

This process consists of major prework involving in-depth analysis of demand and supply as well as input from finance and senior leadership. The work eventually comes together at an executive S&OP meeting. Although the executive S&OP meeting

FIGURE 5-1

Demand-supply integration (DSI)

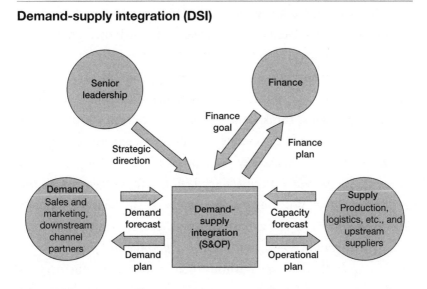

Source: Mark Moon, PhD, University of Tennessee. January 2008. Used with permission.

makes key final decisions, our studies have shown that at least 75 percent of the operating decisions are made in advance at pre-meetings involving personnel lower in the organization.

Many firms use the S&OP process to address myriad cross-functional issues, such as those discussed earlier in the chapter. The meeting may be the only place where all key functions assemble to address issues that transcend individual functions. The S&OP group is a decision-making body, not just a discussion group.

At the tactical level, decisions can be made about how to enhance demand when supply exceeds demand or when financial targets are at risk. These actions might include increased advertising expenditures, pricing adjustments, or new promotional activity. Or the decisions might focus instead on how to dampen demand when demand exceeds supply, such as reducing advertising, raising prices, discontinuing promotional activity, and giving customers incentives to switch to other products and services. The S&OP process can also involve discussions about strategic issues. For example, when capacity exceeds demand, the forum could discuss opening new markets or expanding distribution outlets.

Demand plans and operational plans are the key outputs of the S&OP process. Demand plans deal with imbalances that occur between the forecast of future demand and the forecast of future production capacity by actively managing demand. Operational plans are also set in motion. These include production scheduling, procurement plans, transportation plans, and all other plans that must be implemented to operate the supply side of the enterprise.

We emphasize three key elements of S&OP forums. First, *decision makers must attend, with visible encouragement by the senior executive.* Without decision makers, the S&OP meetings deteriorate into a review rather than a process for resolving issues. Second, the *senior operating, sales, marketing, and finance executives should participate.* Without their involvement, the process breaks down. The financial perspective must be a key element of the decisions reached. Often, various alternatives are available for resolving demand-supply imbalances, and the financial people must participate to offer their perspective. Third, *the process must focus on strategic issues with disciplined agendas.* In the absence of disciplined agendas, the meeting devolves into firefighting. As one executive observed, "Our S&OP meetings quickly dissolve into expediting meetings, focused only on the crisis of the day. We keep solving the same problems because we never get at the root causes."

Enterprises are often faced with an imbalance between demand for products and services in the marketplace and the ability to supply those products and services. In fact, those two numbers (demand for a product and ability to supply the product) are almost never in balance. When demand exceeds supply, shortages result, expediting costs escalate, customers are often left unhappy, and revenue is left unrealized. When supply exceeds demand, production assets are underutilized, inventories grow, and costs escalate. In addition, enterprises are often faced with demand and supply forecasts that may be more or less in balance, but which do not result in achieving financial goals. All this destroys economic profit. Thus, effective S&OP processes are important decision-making forums to help drive economic profit and shareholder value.

Demand and Supply Integration
Industry Survey

We completed a survey of a hundred twenty-two company representatives in 2008 (see table 5-1; the information in the table focuses specifically on the topic of demand and supply integration or S&OP).

In the survey, only 19 percent are extremely or quite satisfied with their S&OP process and 38 percent are somewhat or

TABLE 5-1

Results of University of Tennessee survey on S&OP processes

Which function takes the lead in the S&OP process?	Sales	11%
	Marketing	13%
	Operations	22%
	Finance	1%
	Supply chain	38%
	Forecasting	3%
	Other	12%
Who is the highest-level executive involved in the S&OP process on a regular basis?	CEO	16%
	COO	5%
	Vice president, sales	8%
	Vice president, marketing	13%
	Vice president, supply chain	20%
	Vice president, operations	7%
	Vice president, finance	NA
	Director	17%
	Other	14%
Describe the level of accountability for the success of the S&OP process	Little accountability	6%
	Some accountability, but not shared across functions	42%
	Some accountability shared across functions	28%
	Good accountability shared across functions	24%
Is the S&OP process a global process?	No effort to make global	29%
	Each region has a unique and separate process	22%
	Some regions share some processes	29%
	S&OP process is global	20%
What is the output of the S&OP?	Demand plan	81%
	Manufacturing plan	60%

TABLE 5-1 (*continued*)

	Financial plan	53%
	Inventory plan	53%
	Marketing plan	32%
	Sales plan	45%
	Promotion plan	19%
How strategic is the S&OP process?	Strategic	20%
	Tactical	35%
	Operational	45%
What is the dominant tool used in the S&OP process?	Forecasting software	21%
	Supply chain planning software	11%
	MRP	4%
	ERP	11%
	Financial planning software	4%
	Excel/Access	43%
Is there access to good data in the S&OP process?	Terrible	5%
	OK	44%
	Pretty good	47%
	Excellent	4%
What metrics are used to measure the performance of the S&OP process?	Forecast accuracy	74%
	Inventory turns	63%
	Customer service	73%
	Cost	49%
	Other	50%
How often does the S&OP process take place?	Weekly	18%
	Monthly	60%
	Quarterly	11%
	Semi-annual or annual	4%
What is the planning period for the S&OP process?	Daily	10%
	Weekly	15%
	Monthly	55%

TABLE 5-1 (*continued*)

	Quarterly	10%
	Annual	7%
Which functions have heavy involvement in the process?	Sales	48%
	Marketing	41%
	Operations	67%
	Supply chain	69%
	Finance	23%
	Forecasting	75%
Has S&OP led to business improvements?	Customer service	91%
	Inventory	74%
	Cost	65%
Are S&OP metrics tied to compensation?	Not at all	6%
	For some people	37%
	For quite a few people	30%
	For most people	28%
How satisfied with your S&OP process are you?	Extremely satisfied	3%
	Quite satisfied	16%
	Satisfied	43%
	Somewhat dissatisfied	34%
	Extremely dissatisfied	4%
What is the most important area to improve the S&OP?	Culture	51%
	Process	29%
	Tools	20%

extremely dissatisfied with it. The source of this dissatisfaction seems to be reflected in the data via four key shortcomings:

1. The CEO and the COO are not involved—in only 21 percent of the cases are the CEO or COO involved in S&OP on a regular basis.

2. Inadequate cross-functional metrics and accountability exist—in nearly half of the cases (48 percent), there are no cross-functional metrics or cross-functional accountability.

3. The process is too tactical, focusing on the problem of the day—the S&OP process is primarily tactical in 35 percent of the cases.

4. Sales and marketing are weak participants in the process—in less than half the cases sales and marketing have heavy involvement in the process. It seems to be most often led by forecasting, supply chain, or operations.

Conclusion

Because the supply chain is a horizontal cross-functional process, it is critical to eliminate the vertical, functional barriers that impede it. Therefore, a strategy to deliver supply chain excellence absolutely depends on cross-functional alignment. Although the cross-functional misalignment malady affects all firms, some are implementing processes, such as S&OP, to better manage the problem. With the support of the supply chain leader, the CEO must be in this game. He or she must set the tone and align objectives to allow his or her company to fight competitors who may already be embracing this challenge aggressively. As one of the five steps toward supply chain excellence, internal collaboration is critical to delivering economic profit. But just as important is collaborating externally with suppliers and customers, which we discuss in the next chapter.

S&OP Assessment Test (Table 5-2)

Scoring

- If you score below three on any item, it is cause for alarm. You must address this in order for the process to survive and be successful.

- A total score of 19 or lower essentially ensures that the S&OP process in your firm will fail. Take aggressive action to improve on all fronts.

- A score of 20–44 indicates that problems exist, but there is hope for salvaging the process if aggressive action is taken. Focus on the problem areas and solicit senior management support to fix them.

- A score above 45 indicates the firm is on the pathway to success. Although there is always room for improvement, this can be core strength for the organization. Build on this strength and leverage the process for an expanding array of cross-functional decisions.

TABLE 5-2

S&OP assessment
Rate your company on a scale of 1–10, with 10 being best

Area	Score of 1–2	Score of 3–8	Score of 9–10	Your score
1. Involvement and support of the senior executive	Senior executive is not involved.	The senior executive is somewhat involved in the S&OP process and checks on its status periodically.	The senior executive is deeply involved, openly and consistently supports the process, and makes sure that there is accountability for success shared by all functions.	

TABLE 5-2 (*continued*)

Area	Score of 1–2	Score of 3–8	Score of 9–10	Your score
2. Accountability for success	There are no credible metrics that are evaluated for performance measurement or compensation.	Some credible metrics exist, but they need to be more visible and shared more widely.	Metrics are clearly defined, credible, and not gamed. Compensation is tied to performance on those metrics and shared cross-functionally.	
3. Strategic nature of the process	The process and meetings are highly tactical. Sometimes S&OP meetings focus exclusively on the "problem of the day." There is little agenda discipline.	A mixture of tactical and strategic items are addressed, and the agenda is followed in a disciplined way.	The S&OP agenda is followed with discipline, and that agenda is focused on the strategic, cross-functional issues required to align supply with demand.	
4. S&OP meetings structure	Attendance is sporadic. Meetings are overly detailed. There are no disciplined agendas.	Attendance and meeting discipline are inconsistent.	There are both a pre-S&OP and an executive S&OP. The meetings are relatively brief and follow a disciplined agenda. Attendance is mandatory.	
5. S&OP tools and support	Data is confusing, overly detailed, and no clear graphics are used.	Data clarity and tool use are being implemented.	The data and graphics used are clear and easy to understand. S&OP software is used if appropriate.	
6. Cross-functional involvement	A key function like sales is totally missing from the process.	Sales and marketing are often present in the meetings, along with the other functions.	All functions including sales, marketing, operations, logistics, finance, etc., are involved deeply in the process and are committed to it.	
			Total	

ACTION STEPS

To slay the functional integration dragon, companies should pursue the following action steps:

1. Give the engineering people strong incentives to create product designs that are flexible and ideally have postponement capability.

2. Make sure that supply chain is at the table when new products are designed and planned.

3. Routinely dispose of slow-moving and obsolete SKUs.

4. Minimize product complexity by having as many SKUs as customers need, but no more than needed.

5. Give sales and marketing people strong incentives to get involved in forecasting and demand management.

6. Take the S&OP assessment test and address the problems it exposes.

6

Collaborating Externally

COLLABORATION WITH SUPPLIERS and customers is the fourth step along the pathway to building a strategy to deliver supply chain excellence. Senior executives and their supply chain staffs should pay special attention to the best practices for collaboration outlined in this chapter to ensure success. Unfortunately, as one executive sadly told us when describing the failed efforts in his firm, "When all was said and done, there was far more said than done." His firm made some fundamental mistakes in its collaboration initiatives. But other companies have shown that success is possible. Through examples, we show how the hard work of collaboration can produce outstanding results.

What Is External Collaboration?

External collaboration consists of a supplier and a customer working together to achieve mutual improvement. That's easy to say, but very difficult to do. In our work with hundreds of firms, there are far more examples of adversarial relationships than collaborative partnerships. In the minority of firms that do collaborate successfully, we've seen three stages in their evolving relationships:

Stage one—This stage starts when both parties recognize the potential power of collaboration, which requires some supply chain sophistication on both sides. Senior executive support and encouragement also is a common factor in early collaborative relationships. And, finally, success in getting started depends on both parties acknowledging that it will involve a lot of time and effort.

Stage two—The companies at this stage have a supply chain strategy with collaboration as one of the core elements. The partners have worked together enough to develop the trust to openly share data and strategies. They have a mutual plan to *sustain* the effort, even as people inevitably change jobs over time.

Stage three—At this stage, the parties mutually develop key performance indicators and jointly measure success as a common group. At the final level of maturity, they agree to equitably share the savings from their joint improvement efforts. Companies that reach stage three have better fill rates, lower inventories, and lower costs, and thus higher economic profit. (The companies in the examples in this chapter have strong elements of stage three.)

The CEO's Role in Collaboration

Firms like Lowe's, OfficeMax, Avery Dennison, Michelin, and West Marine in the examples we discuss next benefit from collaboration, both inside the firm, and with their outside partners. They often see changes in all economic profit drivers such as improved fill rates, reduced lead times, lower inventories, and lower costs. No matter how good the supply chain strategy or how talented the supply chain leader, benefits rarely occur unless the CEO sets the right tone. Almost always, he or she needs guidance from his or her supply chain staff to know what to emphasize to most effectively support supplier collaboration efforts. Without visible support, the CEO may cripple the efforts to meet and surpass competition. Functional alignment, discussed in the previous chapter, is a critical precursor to developing the ability to collaborate externally. As we discussed, the CEO, with the advice of the supply chain leadership, can facilitate the alignment of objectives across major functional areas. The CEO must create an environment for collaboration with suppliers and customers to flourish.

Do CEOs understand their role? The CEO of a multibillion-dollar consumer goods manufacturer said he liked to see friction and tension between functions and encouraged intense debate in his meetings. He further demanded a tough-guy approach with suppliers, encouraging aggressive demands without sharing any information or strategy insights. In our experience, this approach virtually eliminates suggestions for improvements from suppliers, leading to delivery problems, long lead times, and quality issues—all destroyers of economic profit. A small but growing number of CEOs we have talked with see the advantage of cooperation with partners, largely because they hear from their supply chain organizations about the major benefits other firms are achieving. This chapter contains a road map for how senior executives and supply chain leaders can move their organizations toward breakthrough performance by setting the foundation for external collaboration.

Does Collaboration Pay Off?

As part of the revival of the Whirlpool supply chain that we participated in (which we'll examine in detail in chapter 8), one of the cornerstones was to develop collaborative forecasts with its three biggest customers, including its largest customer, Sears.[1] (At that time, Sears represented nearly a third of Whirlpool's revenue in North America.) Whirlpool approached Sears and proposed that the two firms develop a joint forecast. The new process consisted of three elements:

1. Each firm developed the best four-month forecast possible for the business.

2. Both companies compared forecasts at the SKU level and limited their focus to areas where differences between the SKU forecasts for the two companies exceeded 10 percent to keep the time commitment reasonable.

3. At a weekly meeting, Whirlpool and Sears teams together discussed the reason for the differences.

For example, in one situation, Sears believed that a certain washing machine model would sell fifteen thousand units in March. The Whirlpool forecast for the same model was only three thousand units, a 400 percent difference. When the teams discussed the reasons for such an extreme gap, they discovered that Sears was planning a promotion for March that Whirlpool was unaware of. Interchanges such as this, occurring weekly, caused an immediate breakthrough in forecast accuracy. Accuracy at the SKU level improved by nearly 50 percent within a few months.

The Sears-Whirlpool supply chain relationship blossomed over time. The two companies' headquarters were separated only by the waters of Lake Michigan, but they had a long history with no formal contract in place. Executives from both companies joked that "the relationship is like a handshake across Lake Michigan . . . with the trigger finger drawn." But over time, as we participated in many monthly face-to-face meetings, each side grew to trust the other, and together we launched a number of mutually beneficial supply chain projects.

Growing Interest in Collaboration

In our experience, successful collaborative relationships between a firm and its core suppliers are still rare. For every positive example, such as Toyota and its supply base or Procter & Gamble and Walmart, there are far more examples of failure to reach even the first stage of collaboration. Successful collaboration between supply chain partners demands a lot of hard work, with mutual trust built slowly over a long period of time. In our supply chain audits, we see more companies beginning to break through the barriers. Recent discussions in our supply chain forum involving forty leading firms indicate the growing interest in collaboration and an appreciation for its potential benefits. Supply chain leaders in these companies report that some CEOs are starting to appreciate the potential.

Much of the motivation for collaboration stems from the common practice of supplier rationalization. When firms reduce their supply base through a supplier-reduction program, they become more dependent on their core suppliers. Companies quickly realize the importance of becoming a preferred customer to their suppliers. Strong suppliers can decide which of their customers will be the first to get the new technology they develop. A firm's innovation pipeline often depends on a partnership with a few core suppliers. World-class firms know they are only as good as their suppliers. This means pushing the supplier to be the best possible, but with full sharing of information, strategy, and technology.

For example, a large consumer packaged-goods manufacturer developed a new hair product. It offered the product first to a retailer with whom it had a strong collaborative relationship. The relationship allowed the manufacturer to get quick feedback and develop an efficient retail supply chain. The retailer was able to have exclusive access to the new product for six months, which allowed it to establish a stronger presence in the hair-product marketplace. In another example, Procter & Gamble developed a new R&D strategy, called C+D—connect (with the outside) and develop. The goal is for 50 percent of innovations to come from outside suppliers versus 10 percent in 2001. Procter & Gamble in effect depends on its suppliers for much of its innovation pipeline.

Toyota pioneered the collaborative supply chain with the *keiretsu* concept, starting in the 1940s.[2] By the 1980s, supplier collaboration appeared more frequently in other industrial societies, proving that it did not depend on the Japanese culture. This approach clearly contrasted to most American manufacturers' standard approach of that era, particularly the automotive manufacturers, that maintained an adversarial relationship (rather than a collaborative one) with their key suppliers. A confrontational relationship chokes off improvement ideas from suppliers, as they focus only on striving to obey the dictates of their customer.

Successful strategies involving a firm's suppliers currently operate over a wide spectrum. As we interact with the supply chain executives from hundreds of companies through our supply chain audits, projects, and forum meetings, they tell us that they are pursuing a combination of three strategies with their supply base:

1. Supplier rationalization

2. Outsourcing to low-cost countries

3. Supplier collaboration

Based on this feedback, we've learned that collaborative relationships are the most difficult to execute successfully and therefore the least common of the three strategies. Only 10 percent of the firms are truly collaborating successfully with their core suppliers, meaning that they have reached the third collaboration stage defined earlier and together are producing positive bottom-line results for each party.

Technology and Supplier Collaboration

Nothing replaces face-to-face communication in establishing and maintaining a collaborative relationship. However, ongoing transactions between two partners must be hassle-free to avoid creating roadblocks. This should be facilitated with technology. Thirty-nine percent of global companies surveyed use automated supplier communications to streamline the processes between the two partners.[3]

For example, IBM implemented a process with its suppliers that eliminated the purchase order.[4] The suppliers simply commit to maintain a certain level of inventory onsite at IBM. In the past, linkages could only occur between suppliers and customers through complex, inflexible, and expensive computer-to-computer links. But in the early 2000s, Web portals became commonly available, causing a dramatic reduction in the cost of supplier interaction, opening the door for all suppliers to come on board, and removing a potential irritant from developing the true collaborative relationship.

With only a Web browser, suppliers and their customers can interface closely with each other. They can use Web-based tools to update their product catalog; track payment status; receive and track orders; and download forecast, inventory, and supply chain plans from the customer firm. Suppliers can enter automatic shipment notices (ASNs) online. They can download and use the customer's program to print bar-code labels. The system can track receipts and automatically generate a scorecard for each supplier. When a condition falls outside the norm, e-mail alerts can occur automatically.

In 2003, Sears and Michelin received recognition from the Voluntary Interindustry Commerce Solutions Association (VICS) for implementing one of the best collaborations.[5] The companies used a Web portal to share information about Michelin supply and Sears demand and inventory status. Sears also communicated planned order requirements and planned inventory levels to Michelin. Later, Sears added other tire suppliers, so they could manage the overall tire supply for Sears stores. Both Sears and its tire suppliers viewed the information in almost real time, collapsing the time required for decision cycles and allowing Sears to avoid out-of-stocks on tires while reducing inventory 25 percent.

Examples of Successful Collaboration

The following examples identify several factors critical to establishing and maintaining a successful collaborative framework. To summarize, each side must first be mutually committed to the relationship and grounded in the strong belief that the process creates breakthrough results for both firms. This translates into real action, such as longer-term contracts and higher revenues for both parties, bringing about strong mutual dependence. Frequent face-to-face meetings then serve as a foundation for establishing trust over time. Finally, successful joint initiatives cement the relationship. All of this obviously requires much time, effort, and leadership. Next, we discuss successful examples for OfficeMax and Avery Dennison, for Lowe's and one of its major suppliers, and for West Marine and its suppliers.

OfficeMax and Avery Dennison

In 2005, Reuben Slone (one of the authors) joined OfficeMax and quickly saw that the relationship between OfficeMax, the large office supplies retailers, and Avery Dennison, one of its major suppliers, involved a lot of firefighting and an arm's-length communication. Meetings sometimes involved emotional exchanges, with Avery people feeling that OfficeMax people made unreasonable demands, and OfficeMax reacting to the intense pressure of customer complaints about out-of-stocks in its stores. With the sales function at Avery interfacing only with the merchandizing function at OfficeMax, supply chain issues in both companies took a backseat, resulting in poor service, high cost, and high inventory levels. Surprises occurred frequently as actual requirements deviated greatly from forecasts. Confrontations occurred all too often as the firms worked to resolve customer complaints. Past efforts to launch joint improvement projects failed either initially or eventually. Operational issues constantly stalled the efforts to drive sales growth. In addition, the aftermath of a 2003 merger for OfficeMax caused the distractions to multiply.

When the new OfficeMax supply chain team took over (led by Slone), the team members quickly realized that the situation with key suppliers had to change. They decided to become a best customer to their suppliers through a real collaboration process. In Avery Dennison, they found a sophisticated supply chain partner willing and able to tackle this challenge.

OfficeMax first established a supplier development team, which provided key data to Avery through a vendor portal. This served as a foundation to identify issues in a fact-based environment before they became a crisis. The supplier development team at OfficeMax involved representatives from several functions, including supply chain and merchandising. This provided the critical mass to address the tough cross-functional issues. Avery matched OfficeMax's team with its group. It further made a substantial investment in additional people to support the new collaborative relationship, including a customer logistics leader who was supported by analytical resources. The additional people served as the resources needed to launch projects to reduce lead time, improve forecast accuracy, and cut inventory, while at the same time improving customer availability, thus driving economic profit for both firms.

To oversee the process, both Avery and OfficeMax established a joint steering committee responsible for setting expectations, establishing strategic and tactical priorities, clarifying accountabilities, and managing performance to tough new targets for inventory and availability. The steering committee agreed on a set of mutual key performance indicators, including metrics such as:

- In-stock percentage

- Customer line fill rate

- Lead time

- On-time delivery from Avery to OfficeMax

- Avery outbound fill rate

- Order forecast accuracy

- Inventory turns

The first meetings allowed people to get to know each other. As Dov Shenkman, Slone's senior vice president of inventory management, said: "We had to feel each other out and slowly build a level of trust. At the start, even the smallest things took a lot of time, including setting the initial meeting agendas. We had to get beyond the belief that the other party had a hidden agenda to gain information that would help in a future negotiation. We had to do the little things right, like share information and plans openly. We had to look for win-wins. We found that once we took the time to get to know each other, everything went better than expected."

At this point, the relationship had matured enough to undertake another major initiative. OfficeMax leveraged Avery's advanced skills in lean manufacturing to improve operations in its own warehouses. This included an intense focus on cycle-time reduction, employee involvement, and continuous improvement (*kaizen*) activities. Once the initiatives were launched, the companies then implemented a plan-do-check-act (PDCA) process to drive sustained improvement. The plan phase included how the joint supply chain could improve business performance for both companies. This moved into a process, called objectives-goals-strategies-measures (OGSM), that aligned the supply chain teams in both companies on priorities, expectations, and key initiatives. A joint value-stream mapping exercise of the overall supply chain process across both firms then identified the key opportunities for improvement. (Value-stream mapping is a technique to visually display the detail of a process in order to see nonvalue-added activities that should be eliminated.)

Did this process produce bottom-line results? The metrics tell a very good story. In-stock fill rates rose significantly to nearly 99 percent from below 95 percent. Lead times were reduced nearly 60 percent. Forecast accuracy improved by over 30 percent, and inventory turnover increased 9 percent. Thanks to the improved trust, OfficeMax was comfortable with lower inventory levels in general and especially lower levels prior to the critical back-to-school peak. Previously, OfficeMax shied away from such practices, fearing that competitors would "steal" inventory from OfficeMax if shortages occurred. Most importantly, the two firms focused much more on driving growth, rather than reactive firefighting. Both partners realize that even with this successful track record, sustaining the forward momentum will be hard work. They look at collaboration as a journey, not a destination. They know that sustaining the momentum will be as difficult as initiating it.

Slone and Steve Burns, vice president of supply chain at Avery Dennison, both say there were some major lessons that drove the success. They agreed on six valuable requirements that resulted in this successful collaboration:

1. A sophisticated supply chain function in OfficeMax and Avery Dennison

2. Investment in additional people to make the collaboration work

3. Trust and willingness to share data openly

4. Mutually developed and shared key performance indicators

5. A shared vision for improvement (lean manufacturing, in this case)

6. A plan to sustain the progress

Lowe's and One of Its Suppliers

The Lowe's supply base consists of a wide range of companies from small regional players to major global corporations. Managing that group of suppliers is a constant challenge with many problems and crises to overcome almost daily. In 2003, one of Lowe's largest suppliers struggled to provide product on time and damage free. That supplier approached Lowe's with a proposal to collaborate to help improve the process. The Lowe's supply chain organization could have taken an arm's-length, confrontational approach, but instead it agreed to work with the supplier to improve its performance.

This supplier sold over $700 million annually to Lowe's, making the relationship very important to Lowe's and nearly life or death to the supplier. The supplier delivered directly to each of Lowe's stores from its regional distribution centers network, consisting of ten centers. The product flowed from the factories to the regional centers and then on to the retailer's stores. Both firms realized that this service model led to problems on a number of dimensions, with availability and damage not meeting the customers' expectations, despite the manufacturer having a high cost-to-serve model and high inventory levels.

A huge advantage is gained if collaboration is grounded in CEO support, and this had two extremely capable CEOs who trusted each other. Robert Tillman, CEO of Lowe's at the time, was especially supportive of collaborating in the supply chain area. Under their sponsorship, each firm created a team and focused on bilateral problem solving.

There was no question that the supplier needed to work with Lowe's to fix all the availability and damage problems. And Lowe's placed a huge incentive on the table. It promised that once the problems were resolved and performance improved to world-class levels, it would increase purchases 30 percent to 40 percent. With this much at stake, both firms invested major resources in the effort. Subteams were first created to use supply chain practices and six sigma techniques to improve the fill rate.

A new collaborative forecasting process resulted in a major improvement in forecasting errors at the SKU level. The process consisted of weekly calls in which the teams from both companies compared independently derived forecasts. This process operated at the SKU level. Because of all the detail involved, collaboration software initially helped compare the forecasts and display the exceptions for the weekly discussions. Both companies quickly realized that the weekly process of meeting and discussing was the key, not the software. In fact, the collaboration software was later abandoned as they found they could compare forecasts simply using Excel.

Supply and demand integration serves as the foundation for any major improvement in availability, and these two companies were no exception. In support, both firms reorganized their operations. The supplier executed a major supply chain reorganization to better integrate operations and supply with demand in a formal S&OP process. Lowe's did its part as well, with such actions as co-locating its demand planners with its supply planners. Forecast collaboration and demand-supply integration led to major breakthrough improvement in availability.

Subteams also attacked the damage problem. These teams used value-stream mapping for the entire logistics process and identified areas for change. Improvements were made everywhere, from the manufacturer's regional distribution centers to the retail stores. A dedicated subteam trained the stores how to properly handle the product. Another subteam focused on store delivery communications.

Within a year, the initiatives clearly produced enough bene-fit that the companies established a joint savings pool, fed by inventory and cost-to-serve savings from the 2003 baseline. These savings were reinvested in the business, with the retailer increas-ing national advertising and the supplier supporting incentives for the retailer's store sales staff. In addition, the manufacturer supported the migration to the Lowe's warehouse network, help-ing Lowe's fill trucks and increase its store delivery frequency. In addition, the supplier developed an education and training pro-gram to provide expertise on the handling of products in the Lowe's warehouses to avoid damage.

The management teams in both companies told us that the success of this collaboration effort rested on five principles:

1. Senior management support

2. Trust painstakingly built from hundreds of hours working together

3. A consistent, defined supply chain strategy

4. Full sharing of information on a weekly basis

5. Agreement to reinvest the savings for a win-win relationship

This example shows again how the hard work of collabora-tion pays off. Lowe's had the foresight to commit to this col-laborative relationship, avoiding the confrontational style that characterizes so many customer-supplier relationships. Collabo-ration is not easy, both to start and to maintain. It takes a full commitment from each side, but clearly the results are well worth the effort.

West Marine and Supplier Collaboration

In 2003, West Marine made an acquisition that complicated an already complex supply chain.[6] Then CEO John Edmondson understood that his company suffered from a supply chain that he characterized as complex, difficult, broken, and a barrier to success. In-stock rates at the retail stores reached an all-time low. Vendors reacted on a purchase-order to purchase-order basis, with no ability for them to plan and optimize their operations.

Larry Smith, vice president of planning and replenishment, and his team developed a new strategy. The center piece involved increased collaboration with suppliers to get out of this reactionary mode. They decided to try collaborative planning, forecasting, and replenishment (CPFR). The process starts with the exchange of timely, realistic forecast data between the supplier and customer, a somewhat counterintuitive approach to many who had been raised in an era of arm's-length, confrontational relationships. After that, planned replenishment orders are created.

West Marine asked VICS to assist in developing a standard process for it. VICS subsequently updated the process, which is called "Collaborative Planning Forecasting and Replenishment."[7]

West Marine improved its forecasts and began sharing them, starting with twelve core suppliers, and eventually expanding to a hundred fifty. In-stock rates improved drastically as did forecast accuracy, inventory turnover, and cost. Even with this obvious improvement, there were pockets of initial resistance within West Marine, as procurement managers had to make a transition from a confrontational to a collaborative relationship. The collaboration team continually promoted the benefits not only to its suppliers, but also inside the company, learning that success depended just as much on ongoing change management as it did with the new process and technology.

The lessons learned here were very similar to those in the two earlier examples. In addition, the West Marine example demonstrates the need to continuously sell the effort inside both organizations at all levels.

The Secret Sauce in a Recipe for
Successful Collaboration

What ingredients make up the recipe for successful collaboration? What allows two companies to progress through the stages of collaboration we outlined at the start of the chapter? The companies in our examples started with a mutual recognition of the power of collaboration and strong commitment to make it work. This philosophy existed on both sides of the relationship in all three situations. These examples, and many others we've gathered from our interactions with hundreds of companies, confirm that if only one party is committed to collaboration, it cannot succeed. Therefore, the first ingredient is *a strong belief by both potential partners in the power of collaboration.*

The examples show the commitment of both parties to invest in the hard work required to make collaboration successful. Countless hours spent in face-to-face meetings and even the investment in additional people clearly showed the dedication of both parties to the relationship. Given the extensive commitment of time and resources for successful collaborations, they clearly must be limited to a small number of core partners. One senior executive believes that the biggest barrier to success centers on the people assigned. They need to be the best and brightest, the A players. This leads to the second ingredient, *a commitment to invest significant time and resources in the relationship.*

In all the examples, the investment of time and resources led to strong mutual trust and a definition of the right goals for both organizations, leading to shared information, technology, and strategies. Many people on both sides of the relationship trusted each other. Otherwise, the loss of a key individual could severely undermine years of work. A formal plan and documented procedures were critical to maintaining the relationship over time. The third ingredient is *trust, grounded in a documented process to sustain the relationship.*

Once the three ingredients are in place, good things happen. Firms evolve through the three stages of collaboration discussed at the beginning of the chapter. As the process matures to its full level, firms commit to sharing the savings equitably, thereby formalizing the win-win relationship. They develop mutual goals and key performance indicators, and measure their performance together as a team. Finally, bottom-line improvements for both partners fully solidify the relationship. Nothing breeds commitment like bottom-line results.

Collaboration with International Partners

The recipe for a successful collaboration described works for local partners. But can we say the same for the global marketplace? There are many more barriers in a global collaboration relationship. The dimensions of distance, time zones, language, and culture conspire to make collaboration exponentially more difficult. Even tougher than the challenge of distance are the differences in language and culture. English is the common language of business, but few speak "global English" well. (Experts in global English speak slowly and free of accents, acronyms, and idioms, and are culturally neutral.) Cultural issues are even more problematic than language.

Cultural Issues

Most cultures depend on personal relationships, but in a few, such as the culture in the United States, they are not as critical.

U.S. businesspeople are perfectly comfortable getting right down to business without knowing any personal details about their counterparts. The people in some cultures say what's on their minds, and others do not. In China, it's much more important to avoid disagreements than it is in the United States. Some cultures are driven by the clock, and others are not. Some live to work, and others work to live. And, even if words are understood, they may have different meanings in different cultures. A *contract*, for example, has a firm legal meaning in the United States, but may just express initial intent in other societies.

Assuming that all the examples in this chapter prove the critical importance of collaboration, does that mean the firms should reconsider some global business opportunities? Firms must take into account the risk when they decide to pursue global strategies like outsourcing. Abandoning the power of collaboration and the resulting continuous rapid improvement is not an acceptable option. Firms must break the code for collaborating with their global partners, with intense dedication to making it work across cultures. Three steps for building a global external collaboration plan to support a supply chain excellence strategy are:

1. Embrace, do not avoid, the challenge of global collaboration.

2. Accept that the challenge and time required for collaboration will be much greater, at least double the effort. Commit to and plan for the effort.

3. Strive to become savvy in the global environment, and learn and experience other cultures.

Conclusion

The supply chain process extends backward to a firm's suppliers and forward to its customers. Therefore, this fourth step—external collaboration—is a fundamental component of developing a strategy to drive supply chain excellence. Collaboration is not easy, but if a firm follows the lessons from the examples in the chapter, breakthrough results can happen, contributing strongly to economic profit for all parties. Of course, all of the work involved in following these four steps is for naught without a solid process for getting new things done in the supply chain area. We address that critical fifth and last step in the next chapter.

ACTION STEPS

1. Become the "best customer" for your core suppliers by openly sharing information and launching joint improvement initiatives.

2. Learn from the successes of other firms and apply the best practices from the examples in the chapter by committing the time and resources, by openly sharing information, by mutually developing joint performance measures, and by sharing the benefits in a win-win relationship.

3. Work even more intensely on collaborative relationships in the more challenging global environment.

7

Managing Change in the Supply Chain

THE LAST BUT EQUALLY CRITICAL step toward a strategy of supply chain excellence is change management. Everything else is for naught if you don't execute successfully. This chapter gives practical advice on how to increase your chances of success on the path to supply chain excellence. You can find project management fundamentals in many other books, but those references often have a generic orientation. Our focus is on creating an execution plan for your supply chain.

Are Supply Chain People Just Too Busy?

The lives of modern supply chain executives look just like those of other senior executives. They are constantly connected, with little downtime to recharge. They often find themselves at the center of the storm, striving to balance very demanding operational objectives with the need to satisfy customers, cut costs, and help grow revenue. They must find ways to operate successfully today, yet also improve rapidly to be competitive in the future. Improvement means getting projects done efficiently and effectively. Supply chain executives operate in the same maelstrom of competing priorities and limited time as their peers, but with the added responsibility of a much broader horizontal responsibility and less direct control than many other executives have.

Transforming the supply chain to achieve excellence and drive shareholder value requires careful attention to project and change management. Supply chain professionals often find themselves ill equipped to accomplish the task. This stems partly from a lack of disciplined application of project and change management principles, and partly results from simply being too busy to have the time to do the right things. Many supply chain executives we talk with concede that they don't have time to do "it" right the first time and therefore spend their days in a vicious cycle trying to fix problems that could have been avoided. In addition, people don't stay in their jobs long in the dynamic business environment today. All the constant turnover and turmoil raise tremendous barriers to getting things done. Successful execution of a supply chain excellence strategy requires more than just a competent supply chain executive; it requires the involvement and support of the entire senior management team.

Problems with Supply Chain Projects

In our audits, we often hear of supply chain initiatives that lost momentum and died. As any good project professional knows, projects fail for many reasons, from underestimating the size of the project to lack of good project leadership to technical deficiency.

But in our experience, supply chain projects have unique issues that make them particularly challenging.

Fixing the Wrong Thing

A line manager from a manufacturing company told us of a chronic problem in its paint system. Defects such as small dark specks in the paint finish would show up on about 2 percent of the units, causing a huge rework cost for the plant, which produced at a high volume every day. The plant manager could hardly contain his frustration as his team launched project after project in a futile attempt to fix the problem, literally spending millions of dollars on possible solutions. As they later discovered, they were simply treating symptoms, not the root cause, and the defects continued unabated.

One day, out of total frustration, the plant manager gathered his staff and took them on a forced march, inch by inch, through the entire process. They found themselves on the roofs, peering inside ovens, and crawling under conveyor lines. Finally, they discovered a simple defect in a roof vent that was allowing dirty air to enter and corrupt the paint process. Fixing the root cause of black specs in the paint meant fixing the roof vent at a cost of a hundred dollars, not millions. This is just one small example from one small part of a supply chain, but if you amplify this complexity many thousands of times, you can see how difficult it can be to ensure that a strategy for supply chain excellence fixes problems rather than creates new ones.

Despite huge complexity, executives must challenge themselves to ensure their strategy and execution plan addresses the root cause of problems. And in most cases, nothing beats walking the process or "riding the truck" to see firsthand the physical flow. The devil is indeed in the details. Any project is unlikely to be successful if at least the most senior supply chain executive and other members of the senior team aren't getting up, away from the high-level reports, and seeing the lines and processes operating. The project management plan needs to include regular "oversight by walking around" checkpoints to make sure that problems obscured or hidden by quantitative reporting are ferreted out.

Failing to Draw a Line in the Sand

A supply chain project manager from a U.S.-based global company told us that she was asked to take her team from its Chicago offices and undertake a three-month assignment in Sweden in the middle of winter, where it was even colder and darker than in Chicago. The project consisted of implementing a supply chain planning process and system in the Swedish factory. The project came close to derailing her career due to her failure to draw a line in the sand.

When they were well into the project, the Swedish plant manager called her into his office and abruptly made a surprising and devastating demand. Unless the project team could provide "daily regeneration capability" (the capability to completely refresh the database every night), he wanted to kill the project. After much discussion and attempted persuasion, the Swedish plant manager remained adamant that this change had to be delivered.

The project manager left the plant manager's office in a daze and hurried to meet with her team. She asked them how much it would cost to provide the feature the plant manager demanded. The technical team's estimate was four thousand hours. She then asked how much slack existed in the resource plan controlling her team of twenty people; they told her that, in fact, four thousand hours of slack existed, but barely. The team members thought they could rebalance the resources and still get the project done on schedule and on budget.

So she decided to agree to the change, all the while having a very uneasy feeling. When the dust settled, her intuition proved right. The change actually took over ten thousand hours instead of the forecasted four thousand hours and caused the project to be three months behind schedule and 20 percent over budget. Where did she go wrong? What could she have done differently?

As we've seen, supply chain excellence requires an expansive view of the supply chain from raw materials to customers. As a result, projects are so complex that it's easy to let a project grow too big and become unmanageable. Scope management is crucial in any project, but the nature of supply chain projects makes it especially important. In the previous example, the project leader later realized that had she set a new expectation at the time, there might have been some initial disappointment at the corporate office, but nothing like the grief she faced by being three months behind schedule and $450,000 over budget. (And that did not include the personal cost to her team of spending three additional months away from home.)

Inability to Quantify the Benefits of the Change

As we stated in chapter 4, "Benefits not quantified equal worthless benefits." Since most of the cost and inventory in a firm depends on how efficiently the supply chain functions, there are often economic profit benefits associated with improvement initiatives. Yet many supply chain professionals lack a financial orientation and struggle to quantify benefits. Their comfort zone consists of making real physical and process changes and leaving scorekeeping to others. Many supply chain projects have been derailed because the benefits were not clearly measured, articulated, and tracked.

On the other hand, we met one supply chain executive who had a real gift in this area. He had a cost-benefit model in his head and passionately felt that any supply chain initiative must deliver benefits in three critical areas. He said that the initiative must first provide better product availability, followed by working capital (inventory) improvement, and third, cost reduction—all key drivers of economic profit. All the people in his organization learned the drill. If you propose a project to the boss, you had better be able to show him benefits in availability, working capital, and cost, in that order. If you didn't, it was back to the drawing board. The supply chain leader kept his superiors and his subordinates constantly focused on the economic profit prize, absolutely critical to delivering and sustaining complex supply chain projects.

Shortage of Supply Chain Experts

A project manager implementing a new inventory management system estimated that a key expert in the inventory management area would need to spend 30 percent of his or her time on the initiative over four months. Although he documented this requirement in the project plan, he admitted that he failed to get full buy-in from the inventory expert and his supervisor. He said, "I found myself holding the bag at a critical stage of the project. When the crunch hit, they were totally consumed by priorities on their home turf, and the project simply could not proceed without this one guy."

The few key people who have focused supply chain expertise are very scarce, as we discussed in chapter 3. Supply chain projects must be planned around these critical resources. Excessively overloading these scarce resources leads to frustration, missed details, missed deadlines, and often failure.

Significant Risks

Since the supply chain is the lifeblood of the corporation, any changes to it can carry huge risk. As we mentioned earlier, supply chain disruptions can have a devastating impact on shareholder value. One study showed an average 40 percent decline in share price due to the supply chain disruptions in the study.[1] A common blind spot for many firms is the inadequate or nonexistent management of the risk associated with supply chain initiatives. There are numerous examples, but they are especially evident in global outsourcing initiatives.

For example, a dishwasher manufacturer decided to outsource the production of water seals to China. The net savings, considering all known costs, were nearly $.75 per unit and totaled a $2 million in annual savings. But soon after the arrangement was made, the Chinese supplier changed to a different rubber supplier, resulting in a catastrophic problem. The seals made from the new rubber leaked in dry climates, causing a nearly 10 percent failure rate. When the problem was discovered, over 2 million dishwashers had been produced with the defective seal. When the seal failed and the unit leaked water onto the floor, it took an average cost of $125 to fix, which included some compensation for water damage to floors in order to maintain goodwill and to try to salvage the manufacturer's reputation. The total cost to the company was north of $7 million. This one event wiped out savings from the outsourcing initiative for over three years. The company thought it had taken all factors into consideration, but it failed spectacularly in considering the potential risks.

Clearly, it is extremely important that a strategy for supply chain excellence identifies risks and that the change management plan appropriately mitigates those risks. We have been amazed to find that it is extremely rare in most of the hundreds of firms we have worked with. For example, when companies analyze outsourcing decisions, they fall into three categories:

- Category one (35 percent)—the company looks at unit cost plus transportation only.

- Category two (55 percent)—the company includes inventory as part of the assessment.

- Category three (10 percent)—the company adds a risk assessment.

In other words, 90 percent of the firms do *not* consider risk when outsourcing production. Yet sourcing offshore carries myriad additional risks such as political instability, port disruptions, currency swings, demand swings, and so on. Unforeseen events occur more frequently in the very long global supply chains, as shown by the following examples:

- In July 2006, 4,700 Mazdas were trapped in a ship listing on its side off Alaska's Aleutian Islands.[2] As a result, inventory stood at twenty-one days of sales (DOS), versus the target of sixty-five DOS, creating a severe availability problem. (That's $103 million in cars lost.)

- In two separate incidents in 1992 and 2002, 113,000 Nike sneakers were lost and are still washing up all over beaches in the Pacific Northwest.[3]

- Ten thousand containers fall off ships annually. Although this is less than 1 percent of total container volume, the 1 percent lost can be enormously disruptive if it's your "efficient" supply chain.[4]

- In 2007, there were 275 pirate attacks on commercial shipping, which increased through 2009.[5]

Because of the huge impact on the corporation, supply chain change management plans have to include thorough risk analysis. Plans must include supply chain risks, probability and impact assessments, and risk-mitigation plans. Executing this process at the beginning of supply chain projects can avoid much pain later.

As far back as the 1940s, engineers developed a well-known approach to identify and prioritize risks using the failure mode and effects analysis (FMEA) approach. The military first used the FMEA approach. It prioritizes risks based on three factors:

1. Seriousness of consequences

2. Likelihood of the problem ever occurring, or frequency of occurrence

3. Likelihood of early detection of the problem

Several firms in our database have successfully applied this approach to the supply chain issues to identify the high-priority risks that require a mitigation plan. They tell us that the framework serves to guide the discussion of risks in a group setting; it's the real power. Given that risk analysis has a large subjective component, reaching group consensus is critical.

Supply Chain Risk at a Food Manufacturer

A food products manufacturer planned to outsource its warehouse operations to a third party. It used a table such as the one in table 7-1 to guide the risk discussion. In brainstorming sessions, the supply chain group identified thirteen risks. Using the approach outlined

TABLE 7-1

Food manufacturer risk analysis

	Risk 1: Safety of food product	Risk 2: Freshness of product
Severity (1–10)	9	6
Probability of occurrence (1–10) High probability = 10 Low probability = 1	2	4
Probability of early detection (1–10) High probability = 1 Low probability = 10	6	2
Priority index (Multiply three items above)	9 x 2 x 6 = 108	6 x 4 x 2 = 48
Recommended action	Enhance testing process	Audit inventory, and ensure stock rotation
Responsibility	Safety engineering	Third party with company oversight

in the table, the group prioritized the risks and eventually decided to launch a mitigation project for the top five prioritized risks. (Only two of the risks are identified in the table.)

Risk at a Durable Goods Manufacturer

A durable goods manufacturing firm faced the problem of determining the risk associated with outsourcing a key manufacturing component to a Vietnamese manufacturer. It used a modified version of the earlier approach, focusing on two factors. It calculated the *probability* of occurrence of each risk multiplied by the *cost* of the occurrence. Although the data is heavily disguised in table 7-2, the analysis done in a group setting looked very much like that shown in the table.

The firm used the analysis in two ways:

1. It made sure that the ROI on the project included the "cost of risk," which in this case was $22.12 per unit.

TABLE 7-2

Durable goods manufacturer's outsourcing risk analysis

Risk	Estimated potential loss, stated as cost per unit	Subjective probability of occurrence	Net loss per unit (Prior two columns multiplied)
Quality failure	$25	.10	$2.50
Safety failure	$100	.01	$1.00
Unexpected demand spike	$30	.25	$7.50
Currency change	$20	.25	$5.00
Intellectual property problem	$10	.25	$2.50
Source disruption Force majeure	$30	.10	$3.00
Port problem	$25	.025	$0.62
		Total	**$22.12**

The outsourcing savings without risk stood at a net $55, which gave it some assurance that the project was still viable, considering the supply chain risk. (It fully recognized the subjective nature of this analysis, but felt it was surely better than no risk analysis at all.)

2. It launched several projects designed to reduce the probability of occurrence of each of the top-five risks.

These two firms are the exceptions in our database of companies. The vast majority of firms have no formal process for dealing with supply chain risk.

The Toughest Part of Change Management

As we stated in chapter 4, people issues are tougher than technology issues. Supply chain professionals tend to underestimate people issues. Supply chain experts, when asked what it takes to successfully implement initiatives, frequently say that it simply requires excellent analysis and a good project plan. Many technically oriented people don't gravitate naturally to the softer issues of communication planning and organizational buy-in. Yet failures in these areas are at the root of many initiative failures.

One firm was installing a warehouse management system but soon ran into a roadblock that caused the project to shut down for several months. The project manager told us that her biggest mistake was to focus on the technical tasks, figuring that the people stuff could come later. She failed to recognize that resistance was building as her team worked in a vacuum. With no communication, the management staff people who operated the warehouse felt totally outside the loop. Their anxiety increased exponentially. It wasn't that the changes were bad; within a year of implementation, the warehouse staff people found they liked them. But fear of the unknown is a powerful force, and that emotion grew and spread as the project proceeded with little communication. When it was nearly time to go live, the backlash grew so strong that it was impossible to proceed. The warehouse management staff banded together and refused to accept the new system. The project leader realized too late that the buy-in process needs to start at the beginning of a project, not the end. This lesson magnifies the importance of the cross-functional, cross-company world of many supply chain initiatives.

Communicate with the Right People

As shown in the previous example, supply chain plans tend to focus on the major challenges of making physical and process changes and don't allocate enough time for communication. But even when communication takes place, it often misses the point.

A project manager leading a major supply chain initiative in a *Fortune* 100 firm thought he had designed the perfect communication plan. He introduced the initiative with a well-crafted thirty-minute presentation to everyone affected. He followed that with a one-hour review to go deeper into the coming change. About a month after the project began, he issued a newsletter that clearly showed the progress made and the benefits to be achieved. Finally, as the project neared completion, he put a six-hundred-word article in the company newsletter. The project manager did many things right, but missed in one important item. He failed to first identify the key individuals in each functional area critical to the success of his initiative, and he failed to design a communication plan specifically for those individuals.

One company we audited estimated that each quarter it communicates over 2 million words to their employees regarding new initiatives. If true, the communication plan in the earlier example amounts to only one-half of 1 percent of that mass of information bombarding these employees quarterly. Unless the communication process precisely targets the key players, it becomes lost in the normal noise of communications in a large enterprise.

In every company, there are people who will make or break a project; this is especially true for complex, cross-functional supply chain projects. These people may be senior executives or critical subject-matter experts embedded in the organization. To manage change effectively, the company must identify these key people and expose them to a *customized* communication plan, with the message depending on the audience. In the extreme stereotype, operations people love to hear about cost-reduction projects, and sales managers get excited about plans to increase revenue. Although never this simplistic, the message must be tailored to the audience for cross-functional supply chain initiatives, as we show in the following examples.

A supply chain executive told us the story of Joe, a brilliant sales planning manager reporting up through the sales organization. The executive suspected that Joe found creative ways to subvert supply chain change initiatives unless he was involved in their planning. It was clear that Joe needed to be involved in the early plans of all new supply chain initiatives affecting the sales area. Not only did this eliminate the problem, but Joe, with his influence within the sales organization, added greatly to the new change effort.

An insightful supply chain project leader described how she achieved full support in the sales and marketing areas for her project, which involved an automated process to flush slow-moving inventory from the company. She first identified each individual in sales and marketing critical to the effort and developed a communications package tailored to them. She then met with each person one-on-one and asked for his or her input. After deciding how to incorporate the suggestions, she again met with each person and described her decisions. She gave them frequent updates as the project progressed. Although extremely time consuming, the process resulted in all key stakeholders in the sales and marketing areas having full ownership. She succeeded in making the initiative to reduce obsolete inventory their project, not a supply chain project.

Plan for Sustaining Change

Most business executives remember initiatives—particularly supply chain projects—that were once big deals but have since faded away and now reside in the scrap heap of "programs of the month." A supply chain executive shared her frustration about a collaborative forecasting project involving the firm's largest customer. Initially very successful, the project languished as key people in both companies moved on to other jobs. As one executive said, "Around here, nothing is colder than yesterday's hot project."

When we polled project managers across many companies, most admitted they did not have a plan for *sustaining* change once the initial implementation is complete (project managers are rarely evaluated on sustaining change, so why should they?). Stories abound of technology projects that were initially successful, but then died when a key individual left the organization or other initiatives were launched. Sustaining change is often more difficult than implementing it in the first place, especially with the cross-functional, cross-company projects required for supply chain excellence. Senior executives should require and support with time and dollars a plan to sustain change after the initial implementation. Such plans often include a provision for refresher training of all users, even those in other functions, and detailed documentation of cross-functional responsibilities in the new process.

Because of the crush of daily demands, supply chain professionals tend to move to the next initiative before ensuring the process change made will be sustained. For example, the CEO of a *Fortune* 500 hard-goods company decided that it was critical to improve forecast accuracy. He told us that this realization hit him when someone accidentally sent him a report showing a 60 percent forecast error at the SKU level. Initially, he said he was very upset that he had never before seen this report, but later realized that this situation had to be the source of many operational inefficiencies in his company. He delegated the problem to a young supply chain vice president who was rising rapidly in the firm. When given the assignment, the vice president realized that he needed help. So he did a little research and brought in the best consultant he could find.

The consultant conducted an audit and found many deficiencies in the process and the systems used. He designed a world-class process and brought in state-of-the-art software. He also convinced the vice president to initiate a forecast collaboration process with the company's largest customers. The plan was outstanding and worked beautifully. Forecast error quickly fell by one-fourth from 60 percent errors to 45 percent errors at the SKU level. Of course, room for improvement still existed, but the CEO told us that he was ecstatic with the process. He said he still demanded additional improvement for the next year. But the young vice president moved on to other problems, assuming this one was on the right track, and was quickly consumed by those other issues. By midyear, the vice president was embarrassed to admit to the CEO that something was very wrong. All the accuracy improvement had been reversed. Of course, they took immediate action to rectify the situation, but by the time the process stabilized, it was too late. Although an improvement trend was reestablished, the average results for the year came in at 59 percent error, almost back to where they started.

What went wrong here? The plan for improvement was technically flawless and had produced early promising results. However, the program missed a key component. The plan to *sustain* the change was missing. When their behavior was no longer monitored, operators gradually returned to their old ways. This process accelerated when new people joined the team. They saw the new process as the consultant's program, not theirs. They didn't under-stand why they were required to do certain things and quickly returned to their comfort zone.

If sustaining supply chain change is more difficult than imple-menting it in the first place, why do project plans for supply chain excellence rarely include a plan for sustaining change? Such a plan should consist of training programs, with a special focus across all functions involved when there is employee turnover. It should also include a periodic audit of the process. And, finally, it should have metrics very clearly posted so that the problems are visible as soon as things start to veer off track.

Senior supply chain executives often have global responsi-bilities, as we discussed in detail in chapter 3. Clearly, manag-ing the supply chain change in a global environment takes on a new dimension of complexity. Cultural differences must be fully included in the change management plan. One thing is certain: change management will take longer in a global, cross-cultural environment.

Conclusion

Driving economic profit and shareholder value through supply chain excellence means focusing on the steps we have outlined in this and prior chapters. Building on these steps means launching projects and completing them successfully. Successful supply chain excellence projects, of course, need to follow all the well-known rules of project and change management. But, with sup-ply chain projects, it is especially important to make sure you are addressing the root cause issues, containing project size properly, and anticipating risk rigorously. Plan for supply chain excellence must recognize the broad scope of the twenty-first century supply chain and embrace the organizational and financial issues that will make or break change efforts. In the next chapter, we pull all the steps together and, with two case studies, illustrate a strategy for supply chain excellence in action. These companies not only developed a strategy but were particularly adept at getting things done.

ACTION STEPS

1. Address the root cause of supply chain problems.

2. Draw a line in the sand and manage project scope closely.

3. Clearly and continuously articulate goals and benefits.

4. Manage and develop a plan to mitigate supply chain risk.

5. Ensure time to communicate properly.

6. Embrace the complexity of managing change in the global environment.

8

Case Studies in Developing and Executing a Supply Chain Strategy

A S WE HAVE STATED throughout this book, shareholder value depends in the long run on creating economic profit, and supply chain excellence is a powerful but overlooked tool for increasing economic profit. Supply chain excellence requires developing and executing a strategy based on the five steps covered in the preceding chapters. This chapter provides detailed case studies of two companies we were involved with—a retailer, Stage Stores, and a manufacturer, Whirlpool. Each of these firms developed and then executed a supply chain strategy that delivered excellence, economic profit, and shareholder value. In both cases, we had more than a front-row view of the considerable challenges. We were part of the team that dealt with them. At

Whirlpool, Paul Dittmann and Reuben Slone were employees at the time and were the insiders in developing and executing the strategy. Stage Stores brought Tom Mentzer onto the board of directors to provide supply chain expertise at a critical point (he continues to serve on the board).

Case Study: Whirlpool

In 2000, Whirlpool North America flipped the switch on a massive new enterprise resource planning (ERP) system, but that technology rollout had less than the desired effect.[1] At the time, Whirlpool shipped close to seventy thousand appliances a day to North American customers. The day after the company went live with the new system, it was able to ship only about two thousand units. Despite many hours of training, when the day came, the line people struggled to use the new system and were confused about where to get key transactional information needed to generate shipments. In effect, they felt as if they were flying blind. As one said, "It felt like we were hurtling down the highway at a hundred miles an hour, trying to steer using the rearview mirror!"

This was an unprecedented disaster in a company with a long and proud history. A barrage of bad press followed. Senior people caucused in conference calls every day at 6 a.m. and 6 p.m. to discuss progress and how to get out of the situation. Eventually, through brute force, a never-say-die company culture, added resources, and numerous work-arounds, shipping recovered to previous levels. But the recovery came with a major cost increase, to say nothing of the many burned-out people who struggled to get through each day. The ERP system survived, and even though the situation improved, the experience of being an example of ERP folly had left scars. At approximately the same time, Whirlpool's number one competitor, General Electric, decided to invest in and significantly upgrade its supply chain operation.

The combination of these two events had a devastating impact on Whirlpool's ability to compete. Cost and inventory increased, and product availability dipped into the 80 percent range versus over 90 percent for its major competitors.

Jeff Fettig, then Whirlpool's president and COO (he is now chairman and CEO), was tired of hearing about spotty service and high logistics costs. Sales had just risen to record levels with the launch of some innovative products and a fortuitous uptick in housing starts. With the rest of the company chugging on all cylinders, there was only one thing holding Whirlpool back: the struggling supply chain. Fettig hired Slone from General Motors and gave him overall responsibility for the supply chain. Slone then brought Dittmann into the mix from a global supply chain assignment at Whirlpool.

On day one of our new assignment, we decided to talk with the sales leadership. They told us, "Your supply chain organization is basically a 'sales disabler,'" along with other unprintable comments. They were justifiably frustrated and had been fighting this battle for too long. We found ourselves on the defensive from the outset. We knew the company was tying up too much capital in finished-goods inventory, yet failing to provide the product availability customers needed. By this time, availability hovered around 87 percent, when it really should have been at least 95 percent, based on industry benchmarks. Costs were excessive, as a result of the number of work-arounds hurriedly put in place to recover from the ERP implementation challenges. Some of our colleagues grimly joked that in surveys on the delivery performance of the four biggest appliance manufacturers, Whirlpool came in *fifth*. Economic profit was being destroyed on all fronts.

Developing the Strategy

We knew we needed a strategy and needed it fast. But we also knew it had to be done right. At the top level, we had one simple idea: get the right product to the right place at the right time—*all* the time. It got complicated very quickly, however, when we faced the scale of the problem. Whirlpool made a diverse line of washers, dryers, refrigerators, dishwashers, and ovens, with manufacturing facilities in thirteen countries. It sold those appliances through big and small retailers and to construction companies and developers that build new homes. The logistics network at the time consisted of eight factory distribution centers, ten regional distribution centers, sixty local distribution centers, and nearly twenty thousand retail and contract customers. To top it off, there were several thousand SKUs.

We decided to formulate a battle plan that would include all five steps toward supply chain excellence, following the process we outlined in chapter 2. We knew that we needed the right people with the right skills; that we would need new technology to supplement the existing ERP technology; that we would have to align closely with sales, marketing, and manufacturing; that we would have to start with our customers and collaborate with them; and finally, we would need a solid plan for execution. Before we could begin to imagine those things, the team had to first look to the future and determine what it would mean to be world class in supply chain performance.

That question could be answered only by focusing on customer requirements first. The approach we used in developing the supply chain strategy was to start with the last link—the consumer—and proceed *backward*. Starting with the customer might seem obvious to some, but the overwhelming tendency in manufacturing organizations is to think about the supply chain as something that originates with the supply base and moves *forward*. Supply chain people naturally find their comfort zone there, since that part of the chain forms their base of experience and control. But the unfortunate effect is that supply chain initiatives often run out of steam before they get to the end point of the customer—their real goal. Whether or not they make customers' lives easier becomes an afterthought.

Our team found that if we *started* with the customer, the customer couldn't be an afterthought. Here, we got lucky. Whirlpool had just completed new research focusing on consumer needs. In the report, we found, not surprisingly, that people value "delivery with integrity," that is, the ability to get it there fast is important, but not as important as the ability to get it there when you said you would. We coined a new slogan: "Give a date, hit a date."

Identifying Priorities of Retail Customers

We next moved upstream in the supply chain. Whirlpool faces fierce competition all over the world. On top of that, it has very smart retail partners that deal with numerous other suppliers. Because these retail customers also buy electronics and apparel and so on, Whirlpool is constantly being challenged by the benchmarks of other, more nimble industries. Technologies continue to evolve, channel power continues to shift, and the bar is constantly raised.

We needed to better understand the desires of our retail trading partners. So we conducted interviews to define requirements by segment. We looked at smaller retailers as well as the big three: Sears, Lowe's, and Best Buy. We asked them about their overall availability requirements, their preferences in communicating, and what they would like to see in terms of collaboration. We asked them about inventory management and how they might want Whirlpool to assist in it. In all, we discovered twenty-seven different dimensions that the retailers used to judge our supply chain capability.

Benchmarking the Competition

Of course, we knew customers' expectations and perceptions are shaped in large part by what others in the industry are doing. So Whirlpool benchmarked its competitors—primarily GE, which at the time was its biggest rival. We obtained cross-industry information and competitive intelligence to make sure we had a broad and objective assessment of supply chain capabilities. Then we mapped what would be considered world-class performance for each of the twenty-seven capabilities and how much it would cost to reach that top level. It turned out that to prevail on every front, we would need to spend more than $115 million, which just wasn't feasible in the climate we found ourselves. It was time for our team to get serious about priorities.

We quickly staked out the areas where a relatively small investment would yield supremacy, usually due to an existing strength like our industry-leading delivery service. We simply decided to cede a few areas (for example, a couple of e-business capabilities) as not that important to our retail partners. We finally settled on a $60 million plan that would meet or beat the competition in all important areas.

Building the Strategy

At this point, we began the hard process of developing the strategy. In building the strategy, we used the five steps, but did not have the luxury of addressing them in sequence. The business situation demanded that we launch as much as possible in parallel. Immediately we focused on building and deepening the *talent* available and getting people in the right jobs. It's a good thing we did, given the lead time required to find the right people. Next we identified the new *technologies* that we would need from warehouse systems to inventory management systems to e-business solutions. Then, starting with our retailers' needs, we developed a plan to *collaborate* with them. At the same time, we knew that we had to build all this on a foundation of *functional alignment*. An essential step along that path of *managing change* was to sell the revolution inside the company.

Internal Collaboration: Selling the Revolution

When to involve internal functions like sales, marketing, and manufacturing in planning a major improvement effort is always a difficult decision. Their time is scarce, and their executives typically don't want to be embroiled in the details. Our team knew it had to have its act together and have a solid plan to which internal customers could respond. We maintained a careful balance between seeking their guidance and selling our vision. For example, we knew we would have to eventually prioritize products and customers, even though the sales function at first wanted great availability for all, with no exceptions.

Our strategy team liked to think we had that mandate from the CEO to get the supply chain fixed. But it wasn't the kind of mandate that comes with a blank check. Like most well-managed companies, Whirlpool will not undertake a capital investment without a compelling business case. As a cost center in the company, the supply chain had to justify every project wholly on expense reductions and working capital improvements. In the highly conservative Whirlpool financial environment, even if our team believed that better product availability would boost sales, we couldn't count that in the business case because it was considered too speculative.

We spent an enormous amount of time talking with the brand general managers and others who needed to eventually support the strategy. The attitude of the sales vice president was typical. Initially, our meetings were confrontational. We weren't coming from a base of credibility, and he challenged everything we said. He had a right to. For example, when we spoke of greatly improving availability while still reducing inventory, he just didn't believe that was possible. The supply chain had done nothing but let him down. We knew we had to persist despite the opposition and justified hostility. We darkly joked, "If he won't let us in the door, we'll go through the window. And if he locks the window, there's always the air vent!" Eventually, his attitude changed, as we showed him how we used his feedback to mold the strategy. He even came to believe that with there was a way to cut inventory and improve availability by being smarter about how we placed inventory in the warehouse network. Finally, he told us that he was pleased with the direction, and we knew then that he felt the strategy was partly his own. A similar story played out in other functions. We found the process of getting functional alignment to be tremendously time consuming, but absolutely essential.

Along the way, we became particularly concerned about cherry-picking. We knew that the first reaction to a multimillion-dollar price tag would be, "OK, what can I get for 80 percent or 60 percent of that total?" We knew the whole strategy—all five steps—wove together, with each part supporting and relying on multiple other parts.

What helped here was the competitive analysis, in which we plotted Whirlpool's capability levels against competitors. We found that we had a real problem with competition in some areas, such as the ability to consolidate complete orders in one load. The competitive instincts of our cross-functional colleagues kicked in. No one wanted to be left behind. We then extrapolated to show how the strategy overcame the gap and put Whirlpool in a number one position.

Getting Approval

After all this work, we needed to get the final approval and then start implementing the project. We knew we had a good plan and were raring to get started. But the final approval meeting of the senior executives was wrapped in a great deal of tension. We knew we were asking for $60 million, funds that included, among other things, money for IT systems and additional people to manage projects. During a period of cutbacks, we were asking for ten times more money than had ever been spent for supply chain process improvements in the past. The funds would have to come from the budgets of the people sitting around the table.

Our team hoped that all the work we had done to communicate and get buy-in was enough to obtain the final approval, but we had some doubts. We knew we had support, but we also knew that the executives around the table had already been through budget cuts. In effect, we were asking them to cut even deeper to fund the new supply chain strategy.

After we presented the strategy to the executive team, Michael Todman, the president of Whirlpool North America, made an anxiety-provoking move by asking each member of his staff to give an immediate thumbs-up or thumbs-down on the investment we had just proposed. We felt enormous relief when we heard the first voice say yes. It was the executive who headed up sales to Sears. The heads of the KitchenAid, Whirlpool, and other brands followed suit. The senior vice president of operations tried to voice his support at the beginning of the meeting, but was asked to wait. Now that it was his turn to vote, he did it with a flourish. "I am fully committed," he said, "to moving our supply chain from a liability to a recognized competitive advantage." Only after Todman had heard from everyone in the room—brands, sales, finance, human resources, and operations—did he cast his vote. With that last yes, the tension broke, and everyone was smiling and nodding. Our team had a sense of triumph, but also trepidation. We knew now there could be no excuses. We were on the hook to deliver some serious value.

Implementing the Five Steps

We quickly launched nine new initiatives, followed by others as soon as we had the capacity. Some were large systems implementations and others involved process improvements. Some examples show how we began to address the steps toward supply chain excellence.

Internal Collaboration

One of the earliest successes in the turnaround of Whirlpool's supply chain was the rollout of a new S&OP process, which took internal functional alignment to a new level. Prior to this, Whirlpool had the typical problem of functional silos. As we look back now, it was about average for the functional alignment problems we see across industry. We installed a process to pull together the long-term and short-term perspectives of marketing, sales, finance, and manufacturing and produce forecasts on which all the participants could base their game plans.

External Collaboration

At the same time, our team focused on outside collaboration with our biggest retailers and launched a collaborative planning, forecasting, and replenishment pilot (CPFR), much like the West Marine initiative discussed in chapter 6. In Whirlpool's case, the collaboration initially focused more on its retail customers rather than its suppliers. The supplier collaboration focus came a little later.

Traditionally, Whirlpool forecast how many appliances it would sell through a retail customer (Sears, for example) to a given market and, at the same time, that customer developed its own forecast. Each company had some information that the other lacked. There was no sharing of forecast information whatsoever. With CPFR, Whirlpool used a Web-based tool to share forecasts (without sharing the sensitive data behind them), and they collaborated on the exceptions. As simple as it sounds, this level of information exchange isn't easy to pull off with busy schedules and a mass of data to analyze, but it's been a real breakthrough. Within thirty days of launch, forecast error was cut in half. Where originally there was close to an 80 percent error rate (which isn't hard, given the small quantities involved in forecasting individual SKUs for specific warehouse locations), soon Whirlpool achieved a 35 percent error rate at the SKU level. To put this in perspective, a one-point improvement in forecast accuracy for the entire company reduces total finished-goods position by $3 million.

Change Management

These were just two of many initiatives launched in rapid succession, quickly hitting two of the excellence steps. As all the initiatives were launched, it was absolutely critical to keep them on track using the principles of supply chain project and change management we outlined in chapter 7. The key was to think big but focus relentlessly on near-term deadlines. To maintain momentum and an image of rapid progress, we organized the change effort into thirty-day chunks, with an average of three new capabilities, or business releases, rolling out monthly—some on the supply side, some on the demand side.

Technology

After six months, we had already done a lot to stabilize product availability and reduce overall supply chain costs. Shortly after, we took a huge step forward by implementing a suite of software products, allowing us better inventory visibility and the capability to set precise safety stocks for each individual SKU at each warehouse location. One year into the overall strategy implementation, Whirlpool achieved historic low inventories and a sustained, high service level. Shortly after, availability improved to a sustained 93 percent availability across all brands and products, a high level for this industry at the time. (Momentum later carried Whirlpool a few percentage points higher.) The team delivered slightly more than promised by reducing finished-goods working capital by 15 percent and improving total cost productivity by 5.1 percent.

Running into Problems

Of course, not everything went smoothly: we managed to commit all of the three deadly sins we discussed in chapter 4 in implementing new technology. We admit that this is particularly ironic, given that technology trouble had been the harbinger of

Whirlpool's woes in the first place. A number of the IT projects fell behind due to expansion of the project scope. After missing a couple of deadlines, we finally put in place a process to relentlessly manage project scope, with disciplined weekly reviews of each project. We also encountered one problem with a beta IT system that surprised us and caused a delayed release as we fought through the software bugs. And although we knew we had to do a lot of cross-functional alignment and selling for each individual project, we underestimated the effort. We scrambled to put change management tasks in our project plans just like any other project task.

Results

Our efforts were all worth it. Whirlpool's customers strongly voiced their approval. A year later, a blind Internet survey of the retailers showed Whirlpool to be "most improved," "easiest to do business with," and "most progressive." After these results came out, the vice president of sales said to the supply chain organization, "You're good now, but more important, you're *consistently* good." It was a turning point in the trade's perception of Whirlpool. Operational results continued to improve. The number of days' worth of finished goods in inventory dropped from 32.8 to just 26. Annual freight and warehousing total cost productivity rose from 4 percent to 7.2 percent. Working capital was reduced by almost $100 million and supply chain costs by almost $20 million. Did this add up to value in excess of the expense the leadership team approved? Absolutely. Total payback on that original investment occurred within the first two years.

Developing Talent for the Future

We certainly did not forget about talent. With all the new initiatives, we knew we needed more people, fast. But we also resolved to make sure we hired the right talent for the future. We were looking for young people with potential whom we felt had a good foundation in the five skills we outlined in chapter 3: a global orientation, the ability to see the supply chain as a system, inspiring leadership, superior technical skills, and good business skills. We recruited young people from companies with strong supply chains and from premier supply chain–oriented MBA programs. We were lucky because the talent drive coincided with a downturn in the industry. On the other hand, it might have been the excitement of a turnaround situation that drew the best and brightest to Whirlpool. These people were not only essential resources to manage the many initiatives we launched, but also the core supply chain talent for the future.

Finally, our core supply chain team members weren't so arrogant as to believe that we didn't need development ourselves. So we assembled a supply chain advisory board and chartered its members to keep challenging us. They reviewed our projects and challenged us to take on more demanding objectives, pushing us closer to the leading edge of the discipline.

Sustaining the Change

Three years into the project, our supply chain team continued to implement new capabilities. This didn't get simpler over time. One of those later projects was the focus on something we called "Plan to Sell/Build to Order." The concept is based on the idea that certain high-volume SKUs—the heart-of-the-line dishwashers, refrigerators, washing machines, and other products that appeal to a broad range of consumers—should never be out of stock. They are the equivalent of a supermarket's milk and eggs; running out of them has a disproportionately negative impact on customers' perceptions.

We formulated a supply chain strategy that allowed identification of these SKUs across all trade partners in all channels to ensure that the replenishment system for the regional warehouses kept them in stock. That constituted the "plan to sell" part of the program. At the same time, for the smallest-volume SKUs, we eliminated the entire inventory and operated on a pure pull basis, with a new, more flexible build-to-order process. The inventory savings on the small-volume SKUs helped offset the costs of stocking up on the high-volume SKUs.

We also worked on the capability to set service levels by SKU. In effect, we recognized that some products are simply more important than others, and that having one availability target for all products, regardless of their strategic importance, does not serve the company. Some products are more profitable; some hold a unique place in the brand strategy. Again, it's easy to grasp the value of being able to vary service levels accordingly, but in a sprawling business like Whirlpool, which ships thousands of different SKUs a day, it was a very difficult thing to accomplish.

Whirlpool is a great company. Of more than fifty purely U.S.-based appliance firms that were doing business in the 1950s, only Whirlpool has survived, growing to the world's largest. By building supply chain excellence, the company has delivered enough economic profit to survive the carnage of this incredibly competitive industry. Whirlpool clearly understands that supply chain excellence will be critical, as it finds a way to thrive in the future.

Does the process of developing and implementing a supply chain strategy work the same way for a retailer as for a manufacturer like Whirlpool? We find that there are far more similarities than differences. Retailers and manufacturers face many of the same supply chain problems, as both strive to provide excellent availability with the lowest operating cost and inventory. In the process, both face similar issues of too many SKUs, too much slow-moving inventory, a complex global physical network, ineffective matching of supply with demand, and so on. In the next case, we focus on a retailer, Stage Stores. It developed a supply chain strategy from 2001 to 2002, based on the same five steps to excellence.

Case Study: Stage Stores

In September 2001, Stage Stores Incorporated (SSI) consisted of small clothing stores in small towns across the southern United States, mostly in the states ranging from Arizona to Alabama.[2] The company's corporate strategy was to build small stores, stocked with brand-name clothing, in towns where little or no competition for brand items existed. This overall corporate strategy required Stage Stores to build a strong bond with medium- to higher-income women and households. The company also wanted to maintain its strong balance sheet and cash flow, along with solid growth in sales and earnings.

When the new SSI CEO, James Scarborough, and a new board took over in September 2001, SSI was just coming out of bankruptcy in the late 1990s. Scarborough was convinced that the corporate and marketing strategies were sound, but to continue to grow shareholder value, the company needed a better understanding and implementation of supply chain management—something he considered critical to his growth strategy for the company.

Talent

Scarborough insisted that his management team include an experienced supply chain management executive, and that the board of directors include a subject-matter expert. Eventually, Tom Mentzer joined the board to fulfill this role. Both Mentzer and the in-house supply chain executive agreed with Scarborough that the problems of the company prior to 2001 had been caused by geographic expansion without consideration of the supply chain management implications. For instance, the company had opened new stores far from the existing distribution center, so that the delivered-to costs to those stores made it impossible to keep prices consistent with customers' expectations and allow the store to make a profit. As a result, new stores were draining profitability from the existing store base and were a big cause of the earlier bankruptcy.

The board consisted of members in the various areas that are typically represented at this level—investor relations, audit, compensation, and governance, for instance. The CEO asked Mentzer to work with the executive team to improve supply chain management and to sensitize the board to the shareholder value implications of supply chain management. The CEO had in place the talent (chapter 3) and the mandate for change management (chapter 7) from the board and down through the organization.

Internal Collaboration

SSI developed an integrated holistic view of the end-to-end supply chain, starting with the customer and going back to the supplier, much as Whirlpool did. From that effort, the company knew that internal collaboration would be essential to achieve the end-to-end supply chain integration. This view served the company well. In a time when many clothing store chains were having financial problems or going bankrupt, SSI maintained a steady growth in sales and earnings from 2002 to 2007 by coordinating traditional functions across its supply chain (see figure 8-1).

Retailers like SSI are generally organized around three functions for each store department—store operations, logistics, and buying—and so have the same problems as any other company aligning functionally. Many retailers consider the independence and often competitiveness of these functions "healthy," but causing a great deal of supply chain problems. Buyers travel the world looking for and buying products they think will sell well in their departments in the store, often without communicating with their logistics and store operations counterparts.

In the past, departmental independence resulted in shipments arriving at an SSI distribution center without advanced notice given to the logistics manager or information on what to do with

FIGURE 8-1

Consistent sales growth at Stage Stores ($ millions)

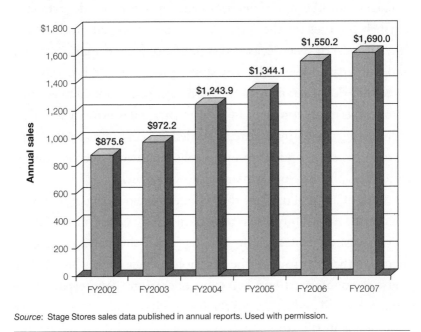

Source: Stage Stores sales data published in annual reports. Used with permission.

the product. The standard approach was to place the product in storage and wait for the stores to ask for it, a practice that incurred costs for inventory and increased needed storage capacity. Likewise, the SSI store operations managers were not given advance notice about the availability of products, so they could not plan how to display and price the product for optimal sale. This practice caused uncoordinated store displays and markdowns on items that could not be moved. All these outcomes adversely affected the economic profit formula from chapter 1 (lower sales, higher cost, and higher capital investment), and negatively affected shareholder value, a big factor in the earlier bankruptcy.

Functional Alignment Through Reorganization

SSI attacked the functional integration problem partly through organizational change. Each department (e.g., ladies, misses, boys, men, shoes, cosmetics) in the chain was given an office in the central headquarters. In that office sat the buyer, the logistics manager, and the store operations manager for that department. Further, bonuses for the three managers were based on the *combined* impact of their decisions on purchasing price, logistics costs, and store markdowns. Thus, by shifting location and rewards, the three traditional retail chain functions were encouraged to coordinate, rather than compete. In a year when sales growth was flat, earnings increased by 8 percent, aided by cost improvements in buying, logistics, and store operations. Improved merchandising meant less product sold at marked-down prices.

One example illustrates the change created by this functional alignment. An SSI buyer was negotiating in Ecuador on $500,000 worth of silver-plated photo albums for the housewares department. Rather than make the decision on her own, she got her logistics counterpart and her store operations counterpart on a conference call and described the potential purchase. "If I can get these items in the stores by September 1," said the store operations person, "I could sell twice that many by Christmas, without a markdown." The logistics manager responded, "To have them in the stores by September 1, I need them delivered to the distribution center by August 1." With this plan, the team agreed it was safe for the buyer to buy twice what she initially intended, knowing they would have them in time to sell them all.

The logistics counterpart coordinated with a trucking company to have the container delivered on time with advance shipment notification (ASN), so he knew when the container had been picked up at the Port of Houston and was en route to the distribution center. The store operations team member planned the in-store display with the confidence that the product would arrive on time. This allowed a reduction in logistics costs because the product was delivered to the distribution center on time. The product could be cross-docked to trucks for store delivery without the labor cost of putting it in storage *and* taking it out of storage. The trucking company was given an inbound shipment to the Stage Stores' distribution center balanced by an outbound shipment to the retail stores, resulting in lower transportation costs. This coordination resulted in the sale of twice as many products as originally planned, all at nonmarkdown prices, with lower inventory and transportation costs. These factors combined to significantly increase the gross profit dollars of the housewares department on which the three members of the team received their annual bonus. Not coincidentally, the factors increased the economic profit for the firm because the profit was achieved with less cost and working capital investment.

In general, across all departments, logistics cost savings at SSI took several forms. A reduction in inbound and outbound transportation costs at the distribution center resulted from a dramatic increase in cross-docking. Again, this meant that arrivals of purchased products could be coordinated with shipments to stores, so trucks were unloaded and the products were remixed to fill store orders and then placed back on the same trucks for delivery to the stores. Since the trucking companies were receiving inbound and outbound shipments, their rates went down. Because 27 percent of all inbound products were now cross-docked, they did not take up expensive distribution-center storage space. Finally, limited storage space at the individual stores was used only for products that were ready to go immediately onto the shelves for sale. All these improvements led to greater sales with lower cost and less inventory, the key components of economic profit.

Functional Alignment Through Performance Measures

SSI also achieved functional alignment by changing performance measures to resolve problems such as one that had arisen from some ingrained buying practices. Buyers were originally compensated for staying within established monthly buying budgets, regardless of store sales. So they bought what they thought they would need at the beginning of the month and then did not buy again until the next month. It was simply convenient to spend their budget allotment all at once, but this meant a whole month's worth of inventory would show up at the distribution center in one week. This caused considerable overtime expense at the distribution center in the peak week and layoffs during the rest of the month. Further, because the buyers often produced inaccurate monthly forecasts, the distribution center ran out of inventory to ship to the stores by the end of the month, leaving the stores with stockouts. To compensate, the stores got into the habit of ordering more than they needed, which resulted in overstocks—and eventual markdowns.

By educating the buyers on the impact they were having on logistics costs and in-store service levels, and changing their compensation package to reward smoothing out of deliveries, the company solved considerable cost and out-of-stock issues. In fact, annual distribution center costs were decreased by over $2 million for workload smoothing, in-store availability increased by 4 percent, and in-store overstocks were minimized.

External Collaboration

Internal functional integration was not going to solve all of SSI's challenges. Scarborough knew that the company needed collaborative relationships with key suppliers and trucking companies and provided the executive leadership and encouragement to make that happen. For example, the board viewed vendor penalties (fines the vendor paid to SSI for nonperformance) as a source of revenue. But Mentzer demonstrated to the board that when a vendor failed to make a delivery to the distribution center, SSI had to expedite the shipment at a cost of $1,500. The vendor penalty "revenue" may have gone up by the $1,000 penalty fee, but SSI was really $500 worse off (and the vendor was $1,000 worse off). Rather than create costs for everyone, it was far better to improve collaboration with suppliers to help minimize late deliveries.

Thus, the board set a goal for the executive team to bring vendor penalties down to zero, through collaboration with the suppliers.

SSI also worked with key suppliers to share critical in-store demand. In return, vendors agreed to hold back shipments to SSI until they were needed. These shipments were always accompanied by an advanced shipment notification, so the distribution center manager, the buyers, and the store managers knew exactly when the next shipment would arrive. This lowered vendor operations costs; SSI overstocks and distribution center shipping and receiving costs; SSI inbound and outbound transportation costs; and store overstocks.

To control transportation costs to its hundreds of stores in over twenty states, the CEO encouraged his chief supply chain executive to work with a few key trucking companies to help decrease deadheading, or miles traveled with empty trucks. For example, they developed a plan to bring full-load shipments to the Jacksonville, Texas, distribution center and to encourage the trucking companies to set up distribution hubs at key locations. The large truck could then make full-truck, long-haul shipments to the distribution center where goods were cross-docked and sent off on a second long-distance run to distribution hubs where goods were reloaded on smaller trucks for short-haul store delivery. SSI also worked with its key trucking companies to obtain freight from other shippers so the percentage of full-truck shipments increased. Cost savings were passed along to SSI, which lowered its cost per carton, and in a win-win situation, the full loads increased the trucking company's efficiency and profitability at the same time.

Technology

The CEO realized that his corporate, marketing, and supply chain strategic plans could not be accomplished without putting the proper operational tools in the hands of his people—tools that allowed buying, logistics, and store operations personnel to communicate with each other, with transportation providers, and with suppliers. With new software, buyers were able to identify the key vendors by department and type of store, enabling more targeted projects with the vendors. Other tools that SSI implemented allowed analysis of sales by product, vendor, department, and store, so it could fully understand the demand patterns hitting the chain. The company went through a detailed search process to select a retail-based ERP suite to accomplish this and avoided the beta technology problem we discussed in chapter 4. The result was a system that allowed anyone in the company to look at sales by category by store, aggregate this information for planning purposes at the distribution center, by vendor for merchandising, and inbound shipments for store operations.

Change Management

All these changes in the operation of the supply chain resulted in major financial improvement. The seventy-five stores opened in fiscal year 2002 had average net sales of $1.5 million, at a normal sales level for a new store. More importantly, the new stores produced an average economic profit of 25 percent of sales (i.e., from selling more with less inventory and lower logistics costs). Figure 8-1 indicates a company with a steady sales-growth pattern. Earnings per share also exhibit a steady growth pattern. In addition, according to the Stage Stores' management, stock analysts complimented the company for its "pristine" balance sheet, with little debt.

Building on Supply Chain Synergy

In the past, supply chain considerations had not been a strong part of SSI's acquisition strategy. This was about to change. SSI's pristine balance sheet allowed it to look around for advantageous acquisitions, and supply chain was front and center. Two companies, Peebles and B.C. Moore, caught the attention of management and the board. Both companies followed a similar marketing strategy to SSI's and were strong geographic matches with SSI. Stores north of South Carolina and Tennessee were Peebles stores, stores in Georgia were B.C. Moore, and the rest were SSI stores.

Redundant Distribution Centers

Before these purchases were made, SSI conducted the usual due diligence analysis, including the supply chain. The supply chain chief executive analyzed the costs of the two Peebles distribution centers (one in South Hill, Virginia, and one in Knoxville, Tennessee), the stores they served, and their viability to serve future store openings. Three conclusions came from this analysis. First, the Knoxville distribution center was redundant to the two larger centers from the combined company (South Hill, Virginia, and Jacksonville, Texas), and was not well-positioned to support future store growth in the Midwest. Serving the same number of stores with one less distribution center allowed a decrease in physical and working capital invested, with no negative impact on sales, resulting in more economic profit.

Operating Efficiencies

The South Hill distribution center moved approximately one-third as many products per year as the Jacksonville center, but at a cost of over $2 million more per year. When this fact was presented to the board with a plan to bring the Virginia distribution center's costs in line with those of the Texas center, one of the financial analyst members of the board said, "That represents a 4 percent accretion to earnings." It was gratifying that the board was beginning to think like supply chain strategists. One of the finance members recognized the impact of supply chain management on earnings, economic profit, and shareholder value.

After the acquisition, SSI management embarked on a two-year project to bring the processes, technology, and training in

South Hill up to the Jacksonville standards. The result was a Virginia distribution center that moved many more products at a considerably lower cost.

Redundant Transportation

Another supply chain insight was that Peebles transshipped product 1.86 million times per year. Transshipment occurred when Peebles received product at the distribution center and, for instance, shipped it to a Richmond, Virginia, store. If a customer walked into a Raleigh, North Carolina, store and wanted that product in the size and color that was at the Richmond store (but not in the Raleigh store), she was told to come back in two days to pick up the product. Peebles then transported the product from Richmond back to the distribution center, reloaded it on the truck to North Carolina, and shipped it to the store. This meant that a product that should have moved from the vendor to the distribution center to the store actually moved from the vendor to the distribution center, to the Virginia store, back to the distribution center, and finally to the North Carolina store. This was a costly way to move almost 2 million products, especially when you consider the fact that the customer might not return after waiting two days.

The logic at Peebles was, "Since we own a private trucking fleet of fifty tractor trailers and they are going to the stores anyway, the movements are free." But, of course, nothing is free. In fact, by bringing demand planning expertise and systems technology to Peebles, SSI cut the incidence of products going to the wrong store by over two-thirds in the first year. SSI also sold the private trucking fleet, which helped finance the purchase of Peebles and decreased the capital cost component in the economic profit formula. It also eliminated the need to manage and maintain a fifty-truck fleet. Through better demand planning, improving distribution center operations, closing a redundant center, and turning store delivery trucking into a variable cost instead of a capital expenditure, SSI saved enough money to pay for the acquisition in a short time (which protected that pristine balance sheet).

B.C. Moore was a small acquisition opportunity. Operating approximately eighty stores in a state where SSI had no presence (Georgia), B.C. Moore was a straightforward cash purchase. Again, supply chain due diligence led SSI to the conclusion that the Moore stores (which SSI would operate under the Peebles name) could be served by the recently redesigned South Hill distribution center, so SSI could close the Moore center. This meant increased revenue from the operation of the eighty stores, without the capital cost of an additional distribution center.

Finally, the purchase of these two companies markedly increased the amount of product SSI bought from vendors. This gave SSI the leverage with key vendors to implement additional win-win savings back up the supply chain.

Economic Profit

By paying attention to the supply chain impact on economic profit (revenue, operating costs, and capital), SSI has been well rewarded in terms of shareholder value. In 2001, its stock was trading at approximately $10, on 20 million outstanding shares (for a shareholder value of $200 million). Steady revenue and earnings growth on a tighter capital base translated into six years of positive economic profit. With two three-for-two stock splits over the six-year period, and a steady policy of shares repurchase, 2007 outstanding shares were 44.3 million, trading in January 2007 at around $30 per share (for a shareholder value of $1.329 billion). Looked at a different way, an investor who bought four shares of stock in July 2001 for $40 would have seen it appreciate to nine shares worth $270 in 2007, a 675 percent return over the six-year period! This return was due in no small part to methodically following the five steps toward supply chain excellence and driving economic profit through the supply chain.

What does the future hold? With the improvement in investor confidence, SSI has plans to drastically expand its store footprint, as well as open a new distribution center to support this expansion and constantly keep an eye on earnings and capital to drive economic profit.

Conclusion

These two cases, a manufacturer and a retailer, demonstrate the power of building a strategy for supply chain excellence to drive economic profit and shareholder value. Such a strategy relies on the five steps covered in the preceding chapters. All are essential; none are optional. If you weave them all together in one integrated supply chain strategy, you will be well on the way to driving shareholder value with your supply chain.

ACTION STEPS

1. Build a supply chain strategy based on the five steps to supply chain excellence: focus on acquiring the right talent, implementing the right technology, collaborating internally and externally, and managing change initiatives with discipline.

2. Keep an eye on the impact of supply chain decisions on the economic profit components.

3. Reward personnel for improving the supply chain. Remember: what is measured gets rewarded and what is rewarded gets done.

4. Continually benchmark competition and best-in-class industries.

NOTES

Chapter 1

1. AMR Research provides subscription advisory services and peer networking opportunities to operations and IT executives in the consumer products, life sciences, manufacturing, and retail sectors. For 2007, the AMR Supply Chain Top 25 portfolio of companies outperformed the market, this time by a wide margin. The average total return of the Top 25 portfolio for 2007 is 17.89 percent, compared with returns of 6.43 percent for the Dow Jones Industrial Average (DJIA) and 3.53 percent for the S&P 500.

2. G. Bennett Stewart, *The Quest for Value* (New York: Harper-Collins, 1999).

3. Working capital is defined as current assets minus current liabilities, but for practical purposes, it is inventory minus account receivables plus accounts payable.

4. Peter F. Drucker, *Classical Drucker: The Wisdom of Peter Drucker from the Pages of the Harvard Business Review* (Boston: Harvard Business School Press, 2006).

5. Gary Balter, managing director at Credit Suisse; David Strasser, managing director at Bank of America Securities. Interview, October 2008, Chicago, Illinois.

6. MAPE is the absolute value of forecast minus actual, divided by the actual, converted to a percentage.

7. Gary Balter, managing director at Credit Suisse; David Strasser, managing director at Bank of America Securities. Interview, October 2008, Chicago, Illinois.

8. *Forbes* Investopedia.com is an excellent source.

9. Calculation done by the supply chain organization at OfficeMax.

10. *Investment Weekly News*, November 1, 2008. (AlixPartners is a global business advisory firm that specializes in improving corporate

financial and operational performance, executing corporate turnarounds, and providing litigation consulting and forensic accounting.)

Chapter 3

1. Charles C. Poirier, Morgan L. Swink, Francis J. Quinn, "Fifth Annual Global Survey of Supply Chain Progress," *Supply Chain Management Review*, October 1, 2007. Access the report at: http://www.scmr.com/article/329710-5th_Annual_Global_Survey_of_Supply_Chain_Progress.php

2. Vicky Gordon, "Leadership Challenges Facing the Next Generation of CEOs: Interviews, 2008–2009," unpublished study. To contact Dr. Gordon, go to www.drvickygordon.com.

3. John Kerr, "Hau Lee-Educator and Consultant." *Supply Chain Management Review*, September 1, 2007.

4. Interview with Vicky Gordon, PhD, senior executive coach, founder and CEO of the Gordon Group, October 2008, Chicago, Illinois.

5. Lao Tzu, Chinese philosopher.

6. Poirier, et al. "Fifth Annual Global Survey of Supply Chain Progress."

7. Interview with Vicky Gordon, October 2008, Chicago, Illinois.

8. Vicky Gordon interview by David Wright in *Leadership Helping Others Succeed: In-depth Interviews with American's Top Leadership Experts* (Sevierville, Tenn.: Insight Publishing, 2006), 11–12.

9. "Supply Chain Talent: State of the Discipline," AMR Research, April 2008, http://www.scmr.com/Contents/images/SupplyChainTalent_StateoftheDiscipline.pdf.

10. Gordon, "Leadership Challenges."

Chapter 4

1. Kevin O'Marah, executive, AMR Research. Interview, January 2009, Boston, Massachusetts.

2. Ibid.

3. Kevin Hendricks and Vinod Singhal, "An Empirical Analysis of the Effect of Supply Chain Disruptions on Long-Run Stock Price performance and Equity Risk of the Firm," *Production Operation Management* 14, no. 1 (Spring 2005): 35–52.

4. Kevin O'Marah. Interview, January 2009, Boston, Massachusetts.

Chapter 5

1. Interview with Scott Roy. Knoxville, Tennessee, March 30, 2009.

Chapter 6

1. Reuben Slone, "Leading a Supply Chain Turnaround," *Harvard Business Review*, October 2004, 114–121.

2. *Keiretsu* refers to a family of companies forming a tight-knit alliance to work together for each other's mutual success.

3. Voluntary Inter-Industry Commerce Solution, "Implementing Successful Large Scale CPFR Programs and Onboarding Trading Partners Business Process Guide," Version 1.0, August 2007, http://www.VICS.org.

4. Thomas Fleck, "Supplier Collaboration in Action at IBM," *Supply Chain Management Review*, March 2008, 30–37.

5. VICS is an industry association consisting of over two hundred companies devoted to improving efficiency and effectiveness of the supply chain.

6. Hau Lee, "West Marine: Driving Growth Through Shipshape Supply Chain Management," Case GS-34 (Palo Alto, CA: Stanford Graduate School of Business, 2004).

7. Voluntary Inter-Industry Commerce Solution (VICS) is an industry association consisting of over two hundred companies devoted to improving efficiency and effectiveness of the supply chain, http://www.VICS.org.

Chapter 7

1. Kevin Hendricks and Vinod Singhal, "An Empirical Analysis of the Effect of Supply Chain Disruptions on Long-Run Stock Price performance and Equity Risk of the Firm," *Production Operation Management* 14, no. 1 (Spring 2005): 35–52.

2. Sharon Silke Carty, "When Cargo Gets Lost at Sea Firms Can See Big Shortages, Losses," *USA Today*, August 3, 2006.

3. Ibid.

4. Ibid.

5. Ibid.

Chapter 8

1. Reuben E. Slone, "Leading a Supply Chain Turnaround," *Harvard Business Review*, October 2004, 114–121.

2. This case was developed primarily from a July 2007 presentation by the CEO to investment analysts and conversations with SSI executives.

INDEX

Note: Page numbers followed by *f* denote figures; those followed by *t* denote tables.

ACKNOWLEDGMENTS

We wanted to make this book as easy to read as possible, yet still provide the substance you need in your journey to supply chain excellence. So, we avoided discussions of abstract concepts and instead illustrated the ideas with many examples and stories. We drew those from our interactions—both as professionals and consultants—with hundreds of companies. The stories, examples, and quotations in this book derive from the database of more than five hundred companies at the University of Tennessee, which houses details from supply chain audits conducted by the University of Tennessee, as well as interactions with attendees of the university's annual supply chain forum.

We would like to extend special thanks to a number of our industry colleagues, including Stern Stewart & Co., Gary Balter of Credit Suisse, Matt Fassler of Goldman Sachs, and David Strasser of Bank of America for helping us draw the strong link of supply chain excellence to shareholder value. We are indebted to executive coach Vicky Gordon and Dave MacEachern of Spencer Stuart for major input to chapter 3 on supply chain talent. In addition, we would like to express appreciation to a number of our colleagues for specific input used in examples, including Kevin O'Marah of AMR Research; Steve Burns, Greg Temple, and Ron North of Avery Dennison; Fred Baumann of JDA Software; Hau Lee of Stanford University; the Stage Stores executive team; Tom Johnson of Michelin; Larry Smith of West Marine; Jay Fortenberry of Honeywell; Scott Roy of Blue Bunny;

and Mike Mabry of Lowe's. We greatly appreciate the support, guidance and insight from OfficeMax CEO Sam Duncan, Office-Max COO Sam Martin, and OfficeMax executives Matt Broad, Dov Shenkman, and Nikhil Sagar.

A number of people provided valuable assistance in getting the manuscript ready for publication. These include Tim Ogden and Laura Starita of Sona Partners. In addition, Jacque Murphy and Kathleen Carr from Harvard Business Press served as critical thought leaders during the book's development.

Finally, we would like to thank our families for their support and encouragement throughout the effort. These include Reuben's wife Carolyn and children Henry and Bridget; Paul's wife Brenda and children David, Kate, and Melissa; and Tom's wife Brenda and children Ashley and Erin.

ABOUT THE AUTHORS

Reuben E. Slone is executive vice president, supply chain, for OfficeMax. Prior to joining OfficeMax, Slone held various executive positions with Whirlpool, General Motors, Federal-Mogul, EDS, and Ernst & Young. *Harvard Business Review* published two of his articles: "Are You the Weakest Link in Your Supply Chain?" in September 2007, and "Leading a Supply Chain Turnaround" in October 2004. Slone received a BS in engineering from the University of Michigan in 1984, where he graduated cum laude.

J. Paul Dittmann is director of corporate partnerships for the University of Tennessee, where he is responsible for the supply chain forum and the Executive in Residence Program, and consults extensively with many firms on supply chain issues. Prior to this assignment, he served as vice president of logistics, vice president of global logistics, and vice president of supply chain strategy for Whirlpool Corporation. He holds a PhD from the University of Missouri and is a member of the Industrial Engineering Hall of Fame.

John T. ("Tom") Mentzer is Chancellor's Professor and holds the Harry J. and Vivienne R. Bruce Excellence Chair of Business at the University of Tennessee. Mentzer is a past president of the Council of Supply Chain Management Professionals. He is one of the most prolific and recognized authors in the supply chain field, with eight books and over two hundred articles in print. Mentzer has consulted for hundreds of companies during his career. He holds a PhD from Michigan State University.